LINCOLN DEL AND OTHER STORIES

A Personal History

Dick Schwartz

D1258316

Dick Schwartz

Table of Contents

Dedication

For my family, past and present

and

Malcolm Gordon (1951-2022)

Acknowledgments

The writing of a book begins long before a pen touches paper. Throughout my lifetime, these people — among countless others — knowingly or not breathed life into mine with their love, support, humor, unique and colorful personalities, courage, know-how and most of all, friendship.

Minnesota:

Malcolm Gordon, Alan Petri, Mike Driscoll (LP), David Troup, Tom Steen, Blair Gershkow, Scott Lipets, Michael Perlman, Michael Dobrin, Bruce McLean, Doug Williams, Gordie "Spike" Rutman, Maggie and Doug Nathan, Ilana and Mike Favero, Laura and Dr. Mark Tanz, Shari and Mitch Grunes, Ellen Joseph, Jerry Strauss, Coaches Ron Petri, Lyle Hanks, Bob Roy, and Roger Anderson; Teachers: Senora De la Pena, Lois Mengelkoch, Dr. Gabriel Davy, Hattie Steinberg, Coach Dr. Robert McCauley; Minneapolis Southwest High School, Star Tribune (Minnesota), my students at Minneapolis Clara Barton Open School and Southwest High School, Professor Gerald Kendahl and D.J. Tice, Commentary editor and columnist, Minneapolis Star Tribune, Professor/Writer Deborah Appleman.

Oregon:

Patty Stone-Wixon and Vince Wixon, Ken Kesey, Billy

Greenberg, Professor John Gage, Jim and Judy Backen,
Jeff at the corner counter stool of Geppetto's, and Dr.
Richard Welton, Professor of anatomy and physiology.

New York City:

Luis Gomez, the anonymous good samaritan who turned in
my forgotten briefcase on the No. 1 subway, Arnie
Schwartz, Ira Berg, Nancy Gelman and Lou D'Amico.

The Netherlands:

Cor Suijk, 1924-2014; Miep Gies, 1904-2010.

Cover art by Anna Mardi Schwartz

About the Author

Dick Schwartz is a retired teacher. He taught high school and college in Ashland and Eugene, Oregon, New York City and Minneapolis, where he currently lives with his wife, Shari.

"Kiss the ground you're walking on."

Arnie Schwartz (Dad), 1969

The web of our life is of a mingled yarn, good and ill together.

All's Well That Ends Well
Will Shakespeare

All the world's a stage, and all the men and women mere players. They have their exits and entrances; And one man in this time plays many parts.

As You Like It
Will Shakespeare

"What matters in life is not what happens to you but what you remember and how you remember it."

Gabriel García Márquez

Part 1

One Year, Four Seasons, A Lifetime

Remembering Heroes and Heartaches From 1968

We survived this tumultuous time fifty years ago, and with a little of Miss Steinberg's "gumption," we can manage to survive again. Fifty years ago, 1968 began this way...

Minnesota had hit the hockey jackpot when the North Stars became ours. My friend Johnny and I nearly hugged each other when our teacher, Miss Steinberg, gave us the green light to write an article about the team.

Miss Steinberg loathed sloppy spellers and sloppy thinkers, wimps and wise guys. Fifty years later, the memory of her red-ink edits and demand for "gumption" intended "to grow you a thick skin" still churns my stomach, for which I am grateful.

Yes. She called it "gumption" back then.

(Note: Tom Friedman, another alum of St. Louis Park High, devoted one of his New York Times columns entirely to Miss Steinberg at the time of her death. He called her "the toughest teacher I ever had.")

All of that journalism skill and character-building were fine by me.

But what mattered most was the chance to rub shoulders with our pro hockey idols, whose tough-guy names added to their star-studdedness: names like Moose (Vasko), Bronco (Horvath) and Cesare (Maniago).

2

On the morning of the interview, Johnny and I showed up at Miss Steinberg's classroom champing at the bit, Johnny with his Polaroid Swinger and me with a sharpened No. 2 at the ready — more determined to score photos and autographs than quotes.

At the Metropolitan Sports Center, long-gone home of our North Stars, a harried public relations guy hustled us into the locker room, pointed at two folding chairs in a corner and ordered us to "wait here and don't touch anything." "And no photographs," he warned Johnny.

Soon our heroes swaggered in from practice, intimidating and indestructible in our eyes. We stared into our blank notepads, peeked at this gods-come-to-life, clueless about how to approach them, completely out of our league, feeling as if Miss Steinberg had thrown us to the lions. "Gumption"? Gone.

Until center, Bill Masterton asked if we were the "school reporters." I probably mumbled, "I dunno. I guess so." Masterton shook our hands and pointed at his teammates. "Go ahead. Ask away." He was a genuinely good guy and, for too brief a time, became my favorite player.

Johnny and I gave it our best shot, but after several excruciating minutes of stammering questions and uninspired responses, Masterton must have surmised our interview was a bust because he summoned Danny O'Shea, one of his more gregarious and cooperative teammates.

3

(We chose to highlight O'Shea in our article. Our high school editors would later print it with the headline, "North Star Player's Daily Life Proves Exciting, Yet Demanding." It would include the eye-opening observation: "After showering and dressing... O'Shea went into the lounge... and watched color TV and smoked.")

Just before that rather nasty PR guy fetched Johnny and me, Masterton slipped us souvenir pucks and allowed us to surreptitiously take one photo each. "Don't tell anyone," he said. I snapped one of Johnny with "Mr. Moose." (Yes. That's what Johnny called Vasko.) Johnny took one of Masterton and me.

I taped the Polaroid image of Masterton and me shaking hands to the inside of my three-ring notebook and enjoyed showing it off. I removed it the day after he died.

You might remember how that happened. On Jan. 13, 1968, during a home game, Masterton's unprotected head slammed onto the ice. It was gruesome. Andre Boudrias, the only North Star (and one of a handful of NHL players) who wore a helmet back then, said it "sounded like a baseball bat hitting a ball."

A photo of Masterton being hauled off the ice on a stretcher so soon after our photo was taken sickened me. I presume to further her "gumption" agenda, and Miss Steinberg assigned me to face my dread head-on and write an editorial in the wake of Masterton's godawful death,

4

exploring why NHL players weren't required to wear helmets. I wasn't emotionally prepared. But this was Miss Steinberg's non-negotiable edict. I melodramatically titled the piece "Death on the Ice."

Miss Steinberg red-penned it "passionate but shallow. Try again." So began 1968.

But just ten days later, the dam broke and sadly, Masterton's tragedy took a back seat when:

North Korea captured the USS Pueblo and took eighty-three sailors prisoner. They were tortured.

Eight days after that, North Vietnam launched the Tet Offensive across South Vietnam; a recently graduated kid from our school was killed in action, along with so many others.

Then the Rev. Martin Luther King Jr. was murdered. Two months later, so was Bobby Kennedy.

Then the Soviet Union invaded Czechoslovakia.

Soon after, we watched the televised brutality between police and protesters outside the Democratic National Convention in Chicago. Third-party presidential candidate George Wallace's running mate, retired Air Force Chief of Staff, Curtis E. LeMay, told us, "… I don't believe the world would end if we exploded a nuclear weapon."

But also that year… "The White Album," "Hair," and heartthrob Olivia Hussey.

1968 ended this way: On Christmas Eve, Apollo 8 astronauts orbited the moon for the first time. Among the thousands of congratulatory telegrams they received, one read: "You saved 1968."

Spring. It's Coming. Because Baseball Is

"I have to absorb the new season like sunlight, letting it turn my winter skin pink and then brown."

W.P. Kinsella, from "Shoeless Joe"

A front-page color photo of Minnesota Twins players beginning their spring training workouts under a warm, cloudless blue sky down there in Florida ("Spring fling," Feb. 15) stirred my juices beyond my lifelong love of the game.

Up here, we're still stuck in winter, spinning our wheels during these frozen, post-holiday doldrums days. My hunch is that most of us have had it with windchills, ice dams, frostbite fears, impound lots, herniated disks and having to do the penguin shuffle on ice that's everywhere. You know this is a particularly nasty winter when the thrill of the "snow day" from school is gone. "Way too many already," I overheard one high schooler lament to another at a coffee shop in the middle of the day, bored out of their minds. Add to all that, the depressing state of the world made uglier than usual because even some folks we voted for are behaving in ways we try to teach our kids not to.

But just when we need her most, Mother Nature is nudging us to awaken. "Time for a change," she whispers at first, her good timing intact as always.

Seems like each one of her seasons inspires her to inspire us. Especially spring, I'd say. Thoughts of imminent spring jump-start our minds and bodies to get off the couch and do things better than the last time we tried. Mother Nature loves do-overs.

"Spring is the time of plans and projects," Tolstoy said. Not to mention the joyful anticipation of a belly flop into a warm lake instead of that heart-thumping polar plunge some are prone to do around this time of year.

You're thinking: A photo of that Twins ballplayer, Jason Castro, suggests all that? I say, Yes! Look at him. He's chiseled and confident, rearing back to throw hard and true. (I swear he's posed like that majestic bronze statue of Zeus, forged in the act of hurling a thunderbolt.)

Look at him. Castro knows what to do, what he needs to do and how to do it. No pretenses. No equivocations. No self-doubts. He's you and me — who we want to be, can be and soon will be. Just as soon as we stash our mukluks, balaclavas, ice cleats and parkas.

Meanwhile, it's still winter. But spring — and with it, baseball — is imminent now. I know that because of the photo (and the coincidental (?) return of that gorgeous cardinal). A. Bartlett Giamatti, American professor of English Renaissance literature, president of Yale University and the seventh commissioner of Major League Baseball, once said, "... The game begins in the spring when everything else begins again."

But let's say baseball isn't your thing. Think about those "everything elses" that matter to you: your son or daughter's (or your?) upcoming prom, planting, spring cleaning (whatever that is, but it's music to our ears), those half-serious, half-in-jest "long time no sees" between you and your hibernating and returning sunbird neighbors, a cold drink in the warm sun, the aroma of fresh-cut grass.

The other morning I opened the front door to get the newspaper. Still cold and gray. Yet another blast of cold air. But this time, I was greeted by a bright, bright red cardinal and his big-time song. Then it started to snow. Later, my street was plowed. But that's OK. Because baseball's back. And you know what that means!

"Spring fling!"

It's front-page news.

Opening Day: Diamonds are a Boy's Best Friend

"Opening Day. All you have to do is say the words, and you feel the shutters thrown wide, the room air out, the light pour in. In baseball, no other day is so pure with possibility..."

Mary Schmich, journalist

... and memory.

On summer days, I would pitch a rubber ball from exactly forty-six footsteps at a square I drew with chalk on the brick schoolhouse wall, dreaming up bottom-of-the-ninth dramas against those hated Yankees while pretty ladies cheered.

In real life, girls biked to our Little League games, where they huddled behind the backstop, pretending indifference toward us by giggling awkwardly at just about everything.

Except for Katie Frye. Katie was confident and composed. Some- times she sat alone in the bleachers to watch us (me?) play. I'd sneak looks at her from our dugout, crazy about her braided hair and the Twins cap she always wore.

Once: Katie watched as I beat out a slow roller to third, a big deal because the other team's burly third baseman was Curtis, the school bully. You tell me: What choice did I have but to race from first to third and slide into him headfirst? Coach Sanderson chewed me out, but, man, was it worth it. After the game, Katie asked me if I was hurt because I might have faked a limp to impress her more. Once: My dad nudged me during the Yom Kippur prayer service and on the QT slid from his breast pocket two tickets to Game

One of the Twins-Dodgers 1965 World Series. Out in the left field, we interrupted our religious fasts and ate hot dogs after we swore not to "…tell your mother."

Once: My parents let me skip school on my 17th birthday to take the city bus downtown to Al Berman's Sporting Goods and buy a Wilson A-2000. I remember on the return trip burrowing my face deep into the glove's deep pocket, inhaling the intoxicating cowhide smell, and admiring Luis Aparicio's fake autograph etched into it. Best birthday ever.

That same spring, I witnessed Coach Dank cutting Markey Schonbloom at baseball tryouts. Markey stood frozen at the gymnasium's center court on that rainy afternoon. His game-worn catcher's mitt dangled from two fingers — an ominous sign. Usually, he pressed it confidently against his thigh, emulating his idol Earl Battey, the great Twins catcher. Coach stood over him, casually holding a fungo bat on his shoulder with both hands and chomping a wad of gum. He mouthed something to Markie, but I couldn't hear the words over the blasts of errant baseballs exploding off the bleachers. Markey looked about

11

to cry or burst with fury. Coach shrugged indifferently and walked away.

I should have gone to bat for Markey, even quit in solidarity with my friend. But I didn't.

Sometimes it's better to regret something you've done than something you haven't.

Once: I hit two home runs in one inning. I had never hit one before and would never hit another. I'm thankful I didn't complicate and taint this one-and-only moment with the whys and hows.

Once: In a near-empty movie theater in Eugene, Ore., on Christmas Day, I watched for the first of countless times my favorite baseball film, "The Natural." It's based on the novel by my then-favorite novelist, Bernard Malamud. Three rows in front of me sat my second-favorite novelist at the time — the hippie-minded tough guy, Ken Kesey — who bellowed a kind of choked-up cheer when the hero, Roy Hobbs… well, watch the film to see for yourself. Preferably on the eve of Opening Day. You won't be sorry.

Once: On a whim, I bought a beat-up roll-top desk at a stoop sale in Brooklyn. Removing its warped backing, I found an "I Like Ike" campaign button, subway tokens and a scrap of paper with Joe DiMaggio's autograph. This one wasn't fake.

Once: I tried out for a powerhouse college baseball team. Their renowned coach was gracious and understanding about "walkon" wannabes like me. He even asked us our names and "Where y'all call home?" Of course, he knew, and he knew we knew he was "only" gifting us with a grand memory to tell our kids. For a couple of hours, we took some swings and ground balls and hob-nobbed with some of the country's best ballplayers, some of whom were destined for the big leagues. I even played catch with a future Chicago Cub, a moment transcended only when years later I did the same with my young son for the first time.

Not long ago, I bumped into Markey at a school plant sale. I strolled with him to his car as he pulled a red wagon filled with flowers. In the trunk lay a heap of catcher's gear, including his game-worn catcher's mitt. I asked him how come he kept it in his car after all these years.

"How come? You never know when you might need it." Opening Day: Let the memories and possibilities begin. Again.

Take Me out to the Ball Game for A Lot More Than Old-Time's Sake

"Baseball, it is said, is only a game. True. And the Grand Canyon is only a hole in Arizona."

George Will

On Apr. 12, 1962, Sid Hartman quoted Minnesota Twins President Calvin Griffith: "We'll play the opening game Friday if it doesn't snow." ("HARTMAN'S Roundup," Minneapolis Morning Tribune).

The game was snowed out.

The Met Stadium crew shoveled a half-foot from the field, teased by the wisecracking "Twins O gram" scoreboard in center field, which said, "Welcome to Twins ski lodge." At game time on Saturday, the temperature was 34 degrees with a 21-mile-per-hour wind. I went anyway — my manhood on the line.

That's because a few weeks earlier, it had taken a hit. My dad had to rescue his nightmare-prone son from the St. Louis Park Theater's Saturday kid's matinee, "The Curse of the Werewolf." I claimed stomachache, but I knew he knew I was faking.

"I'm going to the Twins opener," I announced after that.

"You'll freeze your tuchus off," Dad predicted.

14

Nevertheless, he shelled out the $1.50 for my ticket and made me wear a hat, which I defiantly whipped off when he dropped me at Metropolitan Stadium. I wouldn't wear it because Dad didn't wear one because President Kennedy, his hero, didn't wear one.

Even before the first pitch, I almost called him to bail me out (again). I was glad I didn't, though. Here's why:

Around the third inning, I snuck into one of the umpteen vacant seats within earshot of the Twins' dugout. An old-timer usher caught me but let me stay. He warned me not to make trouble for him, or he'd call my parents. Ballpark ushers did that sort of thing back then.

I heard some Twins cursing at the frigid air. That good guys like Killebrew, Allison, Battey and boy wonder Rich Rollins cussed, surprised but pleased me. Ten-year-olds are bound by Nature to imitate their heroes. Thus, I, too, cussed at the frigid air and, while I was at it, the umpires.

On the drive home, I bragged about how "I snuck into an expensive seat and razzed the umps. "Razzing," I remember saying cautiously. In my house, cursing was forbidden. Once, I said, "damn it." Believe me, I got my comeuppance.

That season we saw Jack Kralick pitch his no-hitter. Baseball lovers will tell you they've hit the jackpot witnessing one, so when first baseman Vic Power caught a towering pop-up with a cocky snap of his mitt for the last

out, I hollered like a seasoned fan, "Holy ****! He *******
did it!!"

Dad didn't bat an eye. The first time you cuss in front of
your dad and get away with it is a giant leap into manhood,
is how I saw it. I think he did, too.

Soon after, Dad cussed in front of me. "I'll be damned,"
he said when JFK proclaimed on the radio, "We choose to
go to the moon in this decade and do the other things, not
because they are easy, but because they are hard... To be
sure, we are behind... in manned flight. But we do not intend
to stay behind, and in this decade, we shall make up and
move ahead."

To many folks, that meant a race to the moon was on
against the Russians. I know I was ready.

Because the only other bad guys I wanted to beat more
than the Yankees were the Russians.

The Yankees won the pennant, though, a heavy burden.
But nothing like when soon after, the Russians blindsided us
with the possibility (likelihood to many) of nuclear war in
what became known as the Cuban missile crisis. For two
agonizing weeks we imagined what our less-than-tactful
fourth-grade teacher, Mr. Brown, assured us would be "a
horrible way to die" (words I'll never forget) — un- til on a
Sunday, JFK made Khrushchev remove his weapons from
Cuba — and like Dad said, "chicken out."

16

The next day, Mr. Brown showed us the Minneapolis Morning Tribune front page, and for the second time, that morning made us recite the Pledge of Allegiance.

An immense relief and optimism I'd never felt before sustained me through that wait-until-next-year winter. We weren't going to die after all. We'd whipped the Russians. This time around, we'd whip the Yankees.

Dad and I played hooky from work and school on Opening Day in '63. He splurged on the most expensive ($3.00) seats and twice more when the Yankees came to town.

That summer was the seventh heaven of baseball and James Bond for my buddies and me and all about JFK for Dad. In the deepest prepubescent voices we could muster, we imitated 007's "Bond — James Bond." We practiced Killebrew's just-try-to-pitch-it-past-me batting stance and Camilo Pasqual's balletic windup in our mirrors and on the Little League field. We marveled when the Twins hit eight homers in one game.

Dad spent the better part of his summer gloating about how Kennedy's "Ich bin ein Berliner" speech "saved democracy."

Then the heartache: The Yankees, not the Twins, won the pennant again. We lost JFK.

I remember nothing about the following winter except for disbelief I'd never felt before that wouldn't go away.

In the spring, a bunch of our parents got together and decided it would be good to let us skip school for the home opener.

The Legend of the Baseball Glove

In late winter 1964, an advertisement in Boy's Life magazine for the one-and-only Wilson Sporting Goods A2000 baseball glove beckoned kids like me in love with baseball and me.

The ad practically dared us to "Tell your dad to help you select a Wilson A2000 at your sporting goods store."

Of course, I did. I pointed out to him that if he really, truly wanted a star ballplayer for a son, the A2000 was a must. And "by the way, Dad, it says right here that Killebrew and Allison play with A2000s."

"Too expensive. Nothing wrong with the one you have," he said, referring to my Woolworth's brand so-called "pro model" glove, the one that looked like Mom's oven mitt.

But it was common knowledge that Dad's winterish mood thawed as each Minnesota Twins Opening Day neared. (He loved baseball, maybe as much as I did). I think that's why on the March morning of my birthday, he surprised me with $36.50 in cash, another 20 cents for city bus fare (round trip) and a note for the school attendance lady excusing me from school after lunch period.

My destination: Al Berman's A and B Sporting Goods in the heart of downtown Minneapolis.

The way I remember it, umpteen beautiful baseball gloves were perfectly aligned along a back wall. A sign read,

"Choose the one that's right for you!" I made a beeline for the array of A2000s, try- ing on each one over and over. Finally, as late afternoon shadows darkened Hennepin Avenue, I left A and B Sporting Goods wearing the "Luis Aparicio" model with its "snap action" and "deep well pocket." I had no need for the box it came in.

Forging the perfect pocket of my A2000 was a joyful obsession. By day I kneaded into the stiff cowhide a concoction of Dads' Barbasol, Mom's petroleum jelly and backyard mud (bedewed with endless shots of saliva) and pummeled the pocket with my fist. By night, I slept with it under my pillow.

Didn't you?

On the first day of Little League practice, I stood (smugly) in center field wearing my A2000, "ready to make impossible catches look easy," as the ad guaranteed.

For three decades, the glove stuck with me through the highs and lows of summer ball, high school, a futile attempt to walk on a college team and years of middle-age slow-pitch softball. Into its fourth decade, once in a blue moon, I'd dig out my now-vintage glove from the pile of family tennis racquets, hockey sticks, rollerblades, soccer balls, skateboards, Wiffle balls and Frisbees and make my young son play catch with me, much to his impatient chagrin.

As we grew older, while he was off adventuring with his buddies, I'd sometimes sit in the backyard sitting with my A2000 and sip a beer until those solitary moments faded away.

Then, almost fifty years after my pilgrimage to A and B Sporting Goods, I had an urge to play catch again because, well, just because. I searched everywhere for my glove — in the basement, attic, closets, garage, under the beds. It was gone. That's all I know. It's not the end of the world when a lifelong keepsake goes missing. But it sure hurts.

On the sly, I'd drive to a sporting goods store and try on the latest A2000s. I thought about replacing my vanished glove with one of these flawless beauties, but each time felt foolish trying them on — a man way-past middle age — and I left barehanded.

Fast-forward to last fall at my fiftieth high school reunion. I'm telling my tale to Bobby, a former teammate. He urges me to look instead at the vintage-like gloves for sale online like he had done. "There's always a bunch of them, but take it from me, they sell fast."

I see a timeworn A2000 that reminds me of my "Luis Aparicio." You can tell it has lived a storied life. Someone (a kid ages ago?) branded into its battered leather "Tumbleweed."

I email Bobby a photo of the glove. He replies, "When you reach our age, you get to do cockamamie things without having to explain yourself. Buy it before someone else does."

I did. Tumbleweed is delivered to me (from Texas!) just before the pandemic hits. I tell some buddies about it. Jerry says, "How old are you? 12?" But another pal, Bruce Mclean, still has his one-and-only glove. He recently has had it restrung at a shoe repair store. (Curious to meet a cobbler who refurbishes baseball gloves, I visit his shop. He says he enjoys restoring them "for guys like you.") Shortly before the stay-at-home order starts, Bruce and I play catch twice. Our haughty throwing motions we honed as kids haven't changed. Neither has the rhythmic sound of the baseball smacking into our gloves. Or the ageless, simple pleasure of tossing a ball back and forth while we talk about Opening Day.

We plan to play catch again soon…

An Homage to the Wilson A2000

"It's your glove, your baseball glove. It's got a soul, a memory all its own, and a future that never fades because it has never let go of the grasp the past has on you and so many others."

Mike Barnicle

Baseball lovers are always telling stories about their new, vintage or, alas, their lost but never-to-be-forgotten baseball or softball gloves. For me and countless others — 17, 27, 47, or 74-year-olds — that means stories about our "top of the heap, king of the hill, number one" A2000.

The glove for the ages.

In a 2008 Esquire magazine article, "Esquire Endorses: The Wilson A2000 Baseball Glove," writer Scott Raab calls it "…the greatest single piece of sporting equipment ever built."

Since 1957, Little Leaguers to pros — and aging codgers like me — would all agree, hands down. Hall of Famer Kirby Puckett once had this to say about the A2000: "As a kid, if you had a Wilson A2000, you had it going on, you know?" He was still playing with an A2000 three-plus decades, 10 All-Star Games and two World Series rings later.

The glove for the ages.

So, down to business. It all begins with breaking in your new glove and sculpting a perfect fit, no matter your age. It takes grunt work, devotion, and loving care — in equal amounts. And scrimp- ing won't do.

(I have fond memories of the 12-year-old me breaking in my first A2000 – a Luis Aparicio model. I describe them in another piece that appears on this blog, "The Legend of the Baseball Glove.") And now, six decades later, Bruce McLean, my life-long friend, and I are breaking in our brand-new 2021 A2000s, his Clayton Kershaw CK22 GM and my Copper and Blonde 1789.

Bruce prefers a straightforward method. He wears it pretty much constantly and pounds (and pounds and pounds…) the heck out of it with his fist and a baseball. And me? Using a slightly more complex method, I twist, pull and stretch my 1789 to soften and sculpt it with generous applications of my own tried-and-true concoction of glove oil, spit, elbow grease and, yes, sleeping with it under my pillow. And all the while, because your baseball glove "has never let go of the grasp the past has on you," I think back to moments way back when that mattered — and still do:

Aug. 22, 1962: In the ninth inning, I'm clutching my A2000 in the third deck, watching the Twins' Jack Kralick pitch his no-hitter. Baseball lovers will tell you they've hit the jackpot witnessing one. So when first baseman Vic Power snags the final out with a cocky snap of his glove, I let fly a volley of joyful expletives, including, "Holy ****! He ******* did it!" It's the first time Dad hears his son swear. He doesn't bat an eye. But cheers turn to tears when we get back to our car—no A2000. In my uninhibited jubilation, I've left it in the ballpark.

I never knew my dad could outrun me. But he does, non-stop through the parking lot and backs up the ramps to the third deck. There, under my seat, only a bit worse for wear among soggy peanut shells and mustard-stained hot dog wrapping, it lies. My sense of relief (and guilt) is indescribable.

That same summer, I'm on the road with Dad for his job. Nearing Milwaukee, he surprises me with tickets to a Cardinals - Braves game, it's "Camera Night." We don't have a camera, but we walk onto the infield anyway. And no one stops me when I wander into the Braves' vacant dugout. Out of nowhere, it seems, the great third baseman Eddie Mathews sits down next to me. He asks me who's my favorite ballplayer. I'm stunned, near tears, and, of course, tongue-tied. But Mathews rescues me when he takes my Luis Aparicio A2000 from me without asking and puts it on. "I'll bet it's Aparicio," he says.

Oct. 6, 1965: Dad hustles me out of the service at our synagogue. With a wink and a grin, he surreptitiously pulls out from his breast pocket two $8.00 tickets for Game One of the World Series - Twins vs. Dodgers. As we speed off to

25

Metropolitan Stadium, he reaches under the car seat and hands me my A2000. Do I care one iota about the odd looks I receive at the ballpark for wearing a fancy blue suit and tie and clutching a baseball glove? Of course, I'm at the World Series with the two things that matter most to me: My dad and my A2000.

How amazingly vivid those images come to life while I break in my latest A2000 now. So is that classic Wilson Sporting Goods advertisement in Boys' Life magazine that started my love affair with the A2000, the one trying to charm and tantalize 12-year-old with: "ARE YOU READY FOR A MAJOR LEAGUE GLOVE?"

You bet I was — and still am.

I meet up with Bruce at the Fern Hill School ball field. This time some buddies will join us with their own worn, storied gloves.

Even more, will join us next time. And more after that. And each time, we'll show off the progress we've made, breaking in our A2000s like the proud (and smug) adolescents we once were.

Some things don't change.

Theater's Saturday kids matinee, "The Curse of the Werewolf." I claimed stomach ache, but I knew he knew I was faking.

Bruce declares that even though our playing days are long past, his new A2000 CK22 will "live on." He'll pass it along to his son, who (like father-like-son) is also a southpaw. I've bequeathed my 1789 to my two-year-old grandson. Soon I'll get another A2000 for his soon-to-arrive baby brother. That way, they'll each have their own when my son — their dad — decides the time is right. In Don DeLillo's unforgettable story, "Pafko at the Wall," about Bobby Thomson's "Shot Heard 'Round the World," a man around my son's age says to a kid he's just met sitting next to him at the

Polo Grounds as they witness the now-legendary Brooklyn Dodger - New York Giant postseason game unfold:

"Next time you hear someone say they're in seventh heaven, think of this."

Or for me, this: It's an unseasonably warm and sun-drenched late autumn day. Back on the Fern Hill School ball field, I laugh, tease and reminisce with Troup, Jaffe, McLean, and Mileski, buddies I've known since childhood while we play catch, still so natural and rhythmic for us after these many, many years.

"You're never too old to play catch." Some things don't change.

On my hand, my A2000 feels like my first one did sixty years ago. Perfect.

Prom: All It Took was a Word, Nod, Swipe of Her Hair

We Minnesotans take the idea of "think spring" to heart after four months of darkness and cold, don't we? We rake still-frozen lawns, jog in shorts and haul out the patio furniture at 40 degrees.

And of course, for many, there's prom.

Oh, these kids. The other day my wife and I overheard some high-school dudes plotting how to ask girls to prom. One plan involved a marching band, another a "polar plunge", and another Opening Day at Target Field. My wife, the pragmatic one, said: "Why can't they just go up to her at school and ask her!" That got me thinking. Once...

Way back when there was Jenny. Just watching Jenny swipe her hair from her eyes could make me nearly keel over. Could I dare ask her to prom? Don't roll your eyes, kids, but this is how I did it: In the school cafeteria, I watched Jenny nibble her apple cobbler as she laughed comfortably with her friends, three tables down and one over from ours...

She glanced my way. I stared down at my tray of greasy chicken and Wonder Bread and butter. That went on for a while. Finally, I guess Jenny had had enough. She wasn't glancing anymore. She gazed at me with purpose — steadily and with intent. Jenny meant business. But she did that swiping thing to her hair, and without much thought, I mouthed "prom," to which she responded wordlessly with a single nod. The deal was done.

All it took was one word, a nod, and beshert. That's a Yiddish word that means "meant to be" or, better yet, destiny. Add the exhilaration that accompanies the transition from Minnesota winter to Minnesota spring, and it motivates us to do things we wouldn't ordinarily do.

Then, the prom, as best as I recollect: dinner at the Nankin; riding the elevator to the top of the Foshay Tower; some local band singing their renditions of "Satisfaction," "Get Ready" and "Tighten Up"; our dates swooping in and out of the restroom all evening like flocks of synchronized birds; Jenny's sky-blue dress and white shawl.

But mostly: Jenny and I drove home in the springtime midnight. Somewhere on E. Lake of the Isles Boulevard, I remember our conversation — because even now, when I drive that way, I think about it — going something like this:

Jenny: "Are you going to college?" Me: "Sure. Probably the U if I get in."

"Don't worry. Everybody gets in. What do you want to be?"

"I want to be secretary-general to the United Nations or a teacher. What about you?"

"Me? I hate seeing poor children who are starving. I'd like to help them. Or maybe a TV reporter."

"Girls can't be TV reporters, but you'd be good at it."

"My mom says I have a big nose even though she says I'm pretty."

"I think your nose is fine."

"So, you think the Beatles will break up?"

"No way. They're making lots of money. They're probably millionaires."

"I really love George. He's always been my favorite one."

"I don't think he's that groovy."

"Well, you're not a girl. I like your car."

"It's my dad's."

"I know, but I like it anyway."

"So maybe we can go to a Twins game sometime. You like baseball?"

"I guess. My dad always complains about the Twins when they lose."

"I was at the World Series. My dad pulled me out of services at our synagogue and surprised me with tickets, and we went in our suits. I wanted to see Sandy Koufax pitch, but he wouldn't because it was a Jewish holiday, and he's Jewish."

"Who?"

"You mean you've never heard of Sandy Koufax?"

"No, but I know who Jim Kaat is. He's a pitcher, too, right?" Then, the moment of truth. I walked Jenny to her door. I have no idea why, but I left the car engine running. At the doorstep, I was nervous. Jenny thanked me for a "nice time." Then:

"You know, you never really asked me to go to the prom."

"Sure I did."

"No. You just said 'prom'."

"Then how did we end up going?"

"I knew what you meant, so I nodded. So why don't you make up for it and ask me to a Twins game sometime?"

We faced each other in awkward silence. But there's something about a gorgeous spring night in Minnesota that can make things feel right. And just like that, in the freshness and stars and moonlight, Jenny looked up at me — steadily and with intent, again. It could only have lasted for a second or two. And she kissed me.

Not long after that, as exhilarated and brash soon-to-be-high-school grads, Jenny and I skipped school and went to a Twins game on a picture-perfect spring day.

Oh, the Stories These Graves and Obits Tell

On Memorial Day mornings, Dad loaded us into the station wagon and drove to Fort Snelling National Cemetery. We'd walk casually among the endless rows of gravestones and rarely speak.

When Dad slowed or paused, so did we. I wondered if this private or sergeant or colonel had died in a battle. To pass the time, I made up stories about that.

I know only one person who actually died in battle. He was two years ahead of me in high school. At most, we'd acknowledge each other with a quick "How's it going?" in the hallway. I don't remember whether he was drafted or enlisted, but one day in my senior year, someone said Donny had been killed in a vague country we'd been sort of learning about in social studies — Vietnam. I haven't thought about Donny in a very long time.

Next, we'd drive to the cemetery where our relatives and a lot of people from the old neighborhood are buried. This time we'd make a beeline to particular gravestones. Mom, Dad, and my grandparents kibitzed about the lives of the deceased at their feet and sometimes quietly argued or chuckled about them while my sister and I tagged along behind. We placed stones on their gravestones. Then Dad herded us back into the car, and that was that.

For the remainder of that Memorial Day, we would welcome back summer with a pickup ballgame, shopping, a barbecue, and the Twins game being broadcast in the background.

I don't visit cemeteries much anymore. But I admit that nowadays, being older and all and, as Walter Becker and Donald Fagen of Steely Dan fame lyricized, closer to "the other side of no tomorrow," I peruse the obits in the newspaper frequently. Not just to stay in the know about a bygone friend, acquaintance, co-worker, neighbor, or someone's someone I should know about. I like the tidbits and stories that a well-written obit shares — beyond the sincere and touching but often clichéd accolades about the deceased. Some of my friends think this is a morbid thing to do, but I don't. I'm comforted, inspired, sometimes even entertained having a glimpse into the lives of ordinary people who seemed to have lived extraordinary lives — sometimes with fanfare and glitz, but not always — and joyful, but, of course, not always that either. I think we can assume there's always heartbreak even if it's not written about.

Craig L., who "...once built a UFO detector and alarm under his bed, which the family cat soon set off in the middle of the night." The gentleman who died " ...after a long battle with cancer and a short battle with a black bear" and another grand man who " …was taken from us in the prime of his life at 98."

And Sandi E., who "…casually ignored her maladies in order to give someone a ride to chemo, support a local restaurant or listen to a cassette tape while watching freight trains from her window." Jack B-C-T, who, as his obit tells us, "…was pulled away from us, back into the infinite universe, to bring music, humor, movies …to at least thirty-three galaxies."

The fellow who "was proud of his blueberries and adored his cat, Lily."

And the lady whose obit life story I can't recall right now, except for her name. But that's OK because when I think about her, I smile and feel a little bit better. Her name was Mary Jester.

And Nicole, whose family shared their heartbreaking message to her with us: "…you cried your last tear, read the last of the nasty messages, posts… that no amount of blocking and deleting could remove the damage done. Instead, you decided enough was enough."

Of course, I'm grateful and humbled when soldiers' stories are included. Like Albert M., who we're told survived the Battle of the Bulge and "…slowly over time was able to tell his family stories of the men he fought with, the carnage, fear, bravery, and death that surrounded them."

Dad never articulated to us the purpose of our family excursions to those cemeteries on Memorial Days. He was the kind of dad who left it to us to figure out what he was thinking on our own.

Naturally, as the years passed and family members dispersed and died, those cemetery visits dwindled and eventually ended. I'm disappointed with myself for not jump-starting the tradition with my own family. I guess there were too many enticing sales, day trips, and barbecues to fill the day off from work and school.

But the obit pages are right next to me now. So on to those. Come to think of it, those cemeteries are pretty close by, too. Maybe this Memorial Day, we'll squeeze in a visit.

Maybe I'll look for Donny's gravestone. It's time.

To Honor the Dead, Speak with Them

I'd never been one to talk with the departed.

A prayer of thanks and remembrance at family members' graves,

lighting a yahrzeit (memorial) candle on the anniversaries of their deaths, placing flowers on their graves on Memorial Day — these have always seemed fitting and right.

But talking to the dead? Not me. Until now.

Mom did it. After Dad died, on many mornings, she'd phone me and say, "I spoke with your father last night." Her matter-of-fact playback of their conversations sounded like they could have taken place at the kitchen table: What we kids were up to. Who'd died.

Who hadn't, yet. The checking account balance. What her cardiologist said this time about her weakening heart.

One morning I stopped by her apartment to replace a light bulb and found Dad's wartime letters to her scattered over the dining room table. "I was reading them to your father," she said.

At first, I was creeped out. The one and only time I suggested, "Ma, you're just dreaming," her staid reply spoke volumes: "We talk things over. It's not too late."

After that, I held my tongue. Who was I to say? Even that time she called to say she'd cooked Dad breakfast, I held my tongue. After all, she'd made his breakfast every morning for 60 years. If all this helped her cope with Dad's absence, why not?

This past year my only sibling, Bobbi Jo, lived her final, grueling months in a nursing home. It turns out she'd been talking to our Dad, too. She said she liked reminding Dad about the silly stuff.

When "that awful attendance lady" caught us playing hooky and Dad disconnected Bobbi Jo's Princess telephone and made me scrub the toilet for a week.

How we sneaked from our bedrooms to watch him and his bowling buddies do belly flops into the apartment swimming pool in their boxers.

But dark matters, too. The ones my sister and I didn't know about then: the family's money woes, Dad's lousy breaks, and dashed dreams. And the health scares he and Mom cried about when they thought Bobbi Jo and I were sleeping behind those thin apartment walls.

It's eerie when suddenly you're the last survivor of the family, now the sole keeper of its secrets and memories — some joyful, some painful, some crystal clear, others still blurry — and saddled with questions you were always afraid to ask or never thought to ask, and things you wanted to say, should have said, but now can't.

Then, very recently, out of nowhere it seems, I came upon a novel, "The Phone Booth at the Edge of the World" by Laura Imai Messina. It's about the aftermath of the tsunami disaster in Japan in 2011 when many thousands died in moments. No final I love yous, thank yous, I'm sorrys or goodbyes. It's a story about how "everyone reacts to death in their own way" — one of those ways being the healing power of "talking" to the departed.

In the story, a survivor of the tsunami installs a telephone booth with a disconnected phone inside in his garden near ground zero of the tsunami to "call" his wife, who died that day. Word of the "Wind Phone" spreads. Soon other husbands and fathers, wives and mothers and children wait patiently in line to "call" their dead, too. Like this young man:

"Hi, Mom? Are you there? It's Keita. Sorry I haven't been here much recently. I'm going to juku every night, and on the weekends, I have special classes for the Todai entrance classes. Anyway, how are you? Are you secretly eating sweets over there, too? Oh yeah, and Naoko's in love. Don't ask me who with. I don't know. OK, I'm going now …See you, I'll come back soon, I promise."

The Wind Phone actually exists.

This year on Memorial Day, I'll watch (for the umpteenth time) the final scene of the film "Saving Private Ryan" when the now-elderly Private James Ryan kneels in front of his captain John Miller's grave at the American cemetery overlooking Omaha Beach in Normandy, France:

"To be honest, I didn't know how I'd feel coming back here. I've lived my life the best I could. I hope that was enough. I hope that at least in your eyes, I've earned what all of you have done for me."

I'll be reminded of how Mom and Bobbi Jo's talks with Dad gave them comfort.

At a local cemetery, after a prayer of thanks and remembrance, this time, I think I'll see what it's like to talk things over with my departed family.

Like Mom said, it's not too late.

All Life Long, It's Mom to the Rescue

"A mother is a mother from the moment her baby is first placed in her arms until eternity. It didn't matter if her child were three, thirteen, or thirty."

Sarah Strohmeyer, "Kindred Spirits."

Dads keep you in line. But mothers come to the rescue. She'll snatch you at the last instant from the edge of the dock.

Search for the 17th time for the monster lurking under your bed or behind the curtains. Chase your family dog in traffic and lure him back home with her homemade brisket. Hug you in the emergency room and even tighter when the Wicked Witch of the West turns over that menacing hourglass and tells Dorothy, "This is how long you've got to be alive."

Later, in your adolescence, when the girl you can't live without tells you she assuredly can live without you, a mom will say it's the girl's loss — not yours — and, "By the way, did you notice what an annoying giggle she has?" and, "Personally, I couldn't bare listening to that day-in and day-out. Honestly, honey, I don't know how you did it."

Mom made it her business to bail me out of a slew of "fixes", as she tenderly and sometimes teasingly called them. Call it "enabling" if you must; to her, it was a mother's calling to come to the rescue. To make things OK.

41

For example: On Thursday nights, our high school football team had a nonnegotiable 7 p.m. curfew, in the words of Coach Roy, "to get your heads screwed on straight" for the Friday night game.

Heaven help you if he called your home and you weren't there but instead (he presumed) gallivanting with some "ne'er-do-wells" (his word).

This is what I was doing during one of those inviolable Thursday night bed checks. A bunch of us had gathered in Johnny Neff's basement — we who had been blackballed from an exclusive club of popular guys — for the inaugural meeting of our own club. Earlier, I'd confessed the pain of that rejection to Mom, which is why she smuggled me from our house and drove me to Johnny's right after Dad left for his weekly poker game.

We named ourselves the "Dohboys" or "D.O.H.'s," linking ourselves in perpetuity with the silly-hearted exclamation, "Doh!" (Think of the film actor James Finlayson, Laurel and Hardy's perpetual nemesis, or Homer Simpson.) How glorious and timely it was to laugh and bond with such a merry band of "ne'er-do-wells." Until Johnny's mother shouts from the top of the stairs, "Is the Schwartz boy down there? His mother's on the phone."

"It's Mom. Your coach just called. He wants to talk to you."

"Jeez. What'd you tell him?"

"I told him you were in the shower."

"What do I do?"

"Call him back. Now. Here's his number. Make sure he doesn't hear whatever it is you boys are up to."

"Jeez... Oh, jeez..."

Then Mom said, "You'll be OK." That kind of thing.

Fast-forward past an umpteen more bailouts. In old age now, Mom rediscovered religion, which meant if you needed her on a Saturday morning, you'd find her at synagogue "in my same seat." Too many hip, knee, spinal, and worsening mind afflictions prevented Dad from accompanying her anymore, although I suspect he was more content to sit in his den cigar-smoking, nibbling on kosher pickles and reading the latest Tom Clancy novel.

On one of these Saturdays, he was healing from his most recent surgery in a nursing home.

That's when I received the call from a nurse to please come there now. Why? "Please. Just come, sir," is all she said.

I remember very little about driving to the nursing home, what was said when I got there, and entering Dad's room with the nurse. Nor do I remember much about the drive shortly afterward to Mom's synagogue.

43

But the rest is as clear as a photo you've kept forever. From the back of the sanctuary, I watched Mom. I'd always admired her athletic golf swing and how she could chase down that dog of ours. But now, she was too weak in the legs to sit-stand-sit-stand with the other congregants.

It was a frightening, impossible task to have to tell her face-to-face, right now, that her husband of fifty-four years had just died. No bailout here.

An usher gently tapped Mom's shoulder and informed her that her son was here to see her. She swiveled and saw me, dressed in jeans and a T-shirt and clutching my car keys. She knew right then.

In the quiet of the foyer, Mom's first words to me were, "You'll be OK."

Call It a Case of 'Mother Knows Best'

Soon after Dad had uprooted our family to North Dakota from our lovely Minneapolis neighborhood to chase a business venture, I moped in the dank basement of our bland rambler, tapping the

keys of a dilapidated piano left by the previous owners, hoping the plaintive sound would lead my mom downstairs to observe my misery and offer the comfort I craved. It did.

"Why are you here all alone?"

I whimpered that I didn't know. But of course, we both did. It's impossible for a nine-year-old to hide homesickness.

"I miss my friends, too," she said. And she hugged me while I cried.

So naturally, she bought me a puppy. That's what mothers do, right?

But that was a temporary fix until I found a friend or two, which for reasons I can't remember, seemed to take a long time. It must have pained her when the dog didn't do the trick, and I insisted on sequestering myself in my barren bedroom.

I remember just two things about that room: The view of a frightfully endless wheat field across our newly paved street — and a balsa wood model airplane that perched for the entire year on the narrow wall shelf facing my bed.

The wheat field I'd sooner forget about (but as you can see, I can't). The balsa wood model and the story of how it got there reminds me of a mother's love and understanding for her child. Here's why:

Occasionally my parents' friends from Minneapolis would trek north to visit. Shirley and Manny Kipperstein came often. Back home, I had idolized their teenage son, Howie, who had paid attention to me like the older brother I didn't have but wanted.

On their first visit, Shirley and Manny brought me a gift from Howie — that balsa wood model airplane. Buoyed in spirit because he hadn't forgotten about me, I immediately assembled it in my bedroom while the grownups kibitzed in the den. Never mind that the box had been opened beforehand.

Assembling Howie's re-gifted airplane was a cinch. All it took was slotting a few parts into some others. No need for instructions. But when I finished, one remaining odd-looking part, uniquely soft and malleable, stumped me. Guessing it might be part of the plane's propeller or rudder, I brought the nearly completed model into the living room and asked Mom about the mysterious leftover component.

Why Mom and not Dad? In my family, the protocol was that unless a question involved sports, you went to Mom for answers. So much so that over time Dad's "Go ask your mother" directive became just a pointed finger toward his wife.

Upon my displaying the piece — silence. Then came the unnerving staccato barrage of cryptic questions from Shirley and Manny. Particularly Manny:

"Did you find this in the box?" and,

"Was the box already opened when we gave it to you?" and, "Do you know what this is?" and, to no one in particular, "How could this happen?"

"Yes."

"Yes."

"No."

"How could what happen?"

Mom must have sensed my growing panic and interrupted the interrogation. She gave me a motherly hug, proclaiming emphatically to all that I had done a terrific job assembling the balsa wood airplane, and declared just as emphatically that the mysterious part was, "…the pilot's helmet, of course."

She also commended the balsa wood airplane company for including humanlike authenticity with its otherwise dull as dishwater design. With that, Mom plopped the helmet onto the pilot's balsa head, making expert-like adjustments here and there.

The helmet completely engulfed the pilot's head. But no matter to me.

"There," she concluded. "Done. How's that, dear?"

Returning to my room, I decided never to fly the now-completed airplane but instead to display it proudly on the wall shelf facing my bed. I remember its constant presence providing me with much-needed jolts of self-esteem during that lonely time.

So much so that even after we unexpectedly packed up and returned to Minneapolis and the old neighborhood (it turned out our family's exodus to North Dakota didn't last long; that spring, the fellow who'd lured my father with guarantees of huge profits and a Pontiac Bonneville skipped town), I continued to display the plane. And Mom, proudly and with an odd giddiness, I remember thinking, ushered her friends proudly into my bedroom to admire the model and indulge their own odd expressions of glee.

For quite a while, the balsa wood plane remained a keepsake, a reminder of the comfort and security my mother gave me — even and especially after I learned the truth behind the events of that evening with the Kippersteins:

One day, Jerry, my worldly buddy, spied the model and immediately proposed a trade: the balsa wood airplane for three of his hard-to-get baseball cards: Mays, Maris, and a Yankee team card.

Enticing, but I balked. "Add Koufax."

Jerry counteroffered. "Then pick two of the cards and just gimme the rubber."

"The what?"

He pointed at the condom.

I was clueless. "No. That's the pilot's helmet. But OK." The deal was done. Koufax and Mays for the pilot's helmet.

When I told my mother about the transaction, she smiled, and we had a good talk.

One Father's Tale of Changing Times and Changing Diapers

It was long ago — or was it yesterday — when this dad watched his son playing T-ball, chasing the dog around the yard and smacking into a tree, balancing paper cups on his baby sister's head with

his friends, fidgeting in his first prom tux, leaving for college, coming home again, leaving again, kissing his bride.

Fond memories, for sure.

Recently, I watched him change his own son's diaper. That tops them all. No kidding.

My mother once told us matter-of-factly (and with an odd sense of pride, I think) that Dad never changed a diaper. "Not one. Not ever."

I asked her how come. She said, "Your dad was working or golfing. Was he supposed to change diapers, too?"

"What about at nighttime?"

"I didn't want to bother him."

Had I the nerve to ask Dad why he didn't (wouldn't) change a diaper — not once, not ever — I know he would have said, "Because your mother did, that's why."

Times change. Most new-age dads like me diapered, fed, bathed, comforted, diapered, fed, bathed and comforted our kids no more and no less (OK, maybe a little less) than new-age moms — even though, in my case anyway, my wife (Mom) was the boss of me (Dad) when it came to such matters.

Nowadays, it's more about parents collaborating and synchronizing their down-to the-minute baby-rearing action plan: to let cry or not cry; milk temperature; bedroom temperature; bath water temperature; sleep aid sounds; outfits for the day; outfits for the night, and above all, keeping the baby ON A SCHEDULE.

"Hon," my son's wife says sweetly but with a hint of concern on the speakerphone (she's off partying with girlfriends on a weekend getaway somewhere in the Upper Peninsula), "when did you feed Ben?"

"About 9:30."

"About?"

"Hold on. I'll check my app… No, it was 9:43."

"OK, that changes things. Ben's off-schedule. Feed him and put him down at 12:03. OK, Hon?"

"But if I put him down at 12:03, then…"

And so on, until deliberations conclude with a decision about when to schedule the next diaper change.

How odd that sounds to me. In simpler times, the proper moment for a diaper change was determined mostly with a whiff.

51

That's old school now. More goes into the timing of a diaper change than I am able to follow. "When you were a baby, we knew when..." falls on deaf ears. He's the dad now.

"I've got this, Dad," he says to me. No doubt he does. I smile. This is the same kid who once chased his dog around the yard and smacked into a tree.

I daydreamed about all kinds of improbable scenarios starring my kids when they were young. You know what I mean: a flawless piano recital, a rousing valedictorian speech, a last-second winning touchdown run...

Imagining my son's adeptness and confidence as he changes his son's poopy diaper was not one of those visions. But it should have been.

Watching my son and his son stare at each other in awe as he does that is the ultimate gift for this dad's Father's Day.

Mom made it her business to bail me out of a slew of "fixes", as she tenderly and sometimes teasingly called them. Call it "enabling".

Journeys With My Dad, Who Was All Business, Mostly

My father's job with the Quality Footwear Co. required that he crisscross the Midwest — "my territory," he called it — maintaining discount shoe displays in grocery stores like Piggly Wiggly,

Red Owl and Harley's Foods 'n' Stuff.

In the summer of 1964, he took me with him. I wasn't sure why, and he offered no reason. I was still too young to drive, and since we barely spoke at home, we wouldn't be much company for each other. Nevertheless, off we drove to Wahoo, Kearney, Ottumwa, and dozens more towns in between and beyond, leaving behind my skeptical mother, whom we wouldn't see again until the night of the Great Speech.

Dad put me to work from the get-go. First, I'd tear open the shipment of "fall styles" with my bare hands. I wasn't allowed to use his box-cutter. He said I had to earn that privilege — his version of a promotion incentive.

But I was somewhat placated when he assigned me the responsibility of repacking and labeling the boxes of "summer styles" for shipment back to the Minneapolis warehouse. After inspecting my work, he'd slap each box once and say, "Done" — his stingy compliment in place of "Good job." Still, what mattered more was earning his trust to use the coveted box-cutter. He knew that.

Next, he taught me how to display the shoes properly on Quality Footwear's imitation wooden tables. ("Ladies' shoes in front, then children's, then men's... Smallest sizes in front... Mix your colors and styles... No! Not that way... Tuck the lace inside... Watch me... Now you try.") In my dad's way of thinking, even a Harley's Foods 'n' Stuff deserved a professionally prepared display of discount shoes.

After we serviced the last store for the day, we ate quickly, then took to the road. At first, I dreaded the long hours ahead before TV and sleep. But soon, driving into the night on deserted highways and back roads became an exhilarating trek into the unknown.

This, of course, was from the perspective of a kid who rarely left his sheltered neighborhood, hadn't risked much of anything yet, and whose worldview was pretty much limited to a geography book. Out here, the faint light of a lonesome farmhouse and the creepy shadow of a railroad crossing was the New World to me. "Manning the radio," as my dad called it, was my job in the car. I swiveled the knobs and pushed the buttons with the focus of a co-pilot to find an audible station that we — well, he — liked.

Those were the quirky twangs of the tiny-town Christian and farm report DJs and the local "news anchors" who at first sounded

like they came from another planet. But somewhere in Nebraska or Kansas, those alien voices became more companionable than listening to "I Want to Hold Your Hand" or "Surfin' Bird" for the umpteen millionth time in the middle of somewhere.

For nearly three weeks, I piloted the radio with pride and peonage and had earned station-choosing executive power. But on our last night on the road, when Dad heard the Democratic National Convention on the air, he told me to "lock it in."

"But I've been in charge of..."

"Let's listen to what he says."

"Who?"

"He" was Hubert Humphrey. The "what" was his acceptance speech to run for the office of vice president.

Even us unstudied, goofball kids knew of Hubert Humphrey. He was almost everyone's Minnesota Nice guy. My dad liked him, too, but had remarked more than once that he thought Hubert was sometimes "too much of a softy."

But on this night, he became our Minnesota Tough guy. The man was out for blood as he took aim at Arizona Sen.

Barry Goldwater, the Republicans' severe-looking, nasty-sounding nominee for president.

If you're old enough, you might have listened to or watched Humphrey's Great Speech. His adamant refrain, "But not Senator Goldwater!" each time he called the GOP candidate out for voting "no" on Senate bills, may have sealed the deal for President Lyndon Johnson in many Americans' hearts and minds. (As in: "Most Democrats and Republicans in the Senate… voted for the Civil Rights Act — but not Senator Goldwater!")

Nine times Humphrey blasted him with a "But not Senator Goldwater!"

Nine times.

At first, we listened to the delegates applaud appreciatively. But they caught on: Applause turned to cheers, then into a jubilant frenzy and, finally, at the anticipated moment, they accompanied Humphrey in a near-hysterical "But not Senator Goldwater!"

I had witnessed my dad's response to hysterics just once, two years earlier, when the Twins' Jack Kralick took his no-hitter into the ninth inning and finished it. Dad dutifully stood with wildly cheering fans surrounding us. But, of course, he just applauded demurely.

But this time, at Humphrey's ninth refrain, he smacked the steering wheel and shouted — I mean really shouted —

along with the convention delegates, "But not Senator Goldwater!"

I'm not sure which of us was more startled.

The following night, after my dad had gone to bed, I told Mom about Humphrey's speech and what my dad did.

Then I explained everything Dad had taught me about the discount shoe business and showed her the box-cutter he bought for me in Grand Island, Nebraska.

How I Came to Love Small-Town Life on the Fourth of July

When I'd had my fill of city life, I fled to a small town out West that you've probably never heard of. Family and friends thought I was nuts.

I arrived near midnight on July 1st and drove deserted streets, passed pitch-black storefronts and houses, then checked into an isolated motel. Family and friends were right. I didn't belong here.

The next day, alone and lonely, I sat at their Woolworth's soda fountain and whimpered, "I can't live here." And then, more loudly, "What was I thinking?"

Francine the soda fountain waitress heard me. "About what? "Living here. I can't do it."

She looked me over. "Where you from?"

"Minneapolis."

She said something like, "Oh, the city. You found a place yet?"

"Your Motel 6 for now."

I must have looked and sounded pathetic — lost. I know I felt that way.

"Don't worry, hon'. We'll fix that." Francine telephoned her ex, Rex Love, owner of three small apartments above the Copper Kitchen Café; the next morning, I awoke in a cozy efficiency next door to Francine, Frank, and their twin 3-year-olds. Just like that. Then, long before dawn on the Fourth of July, Frank knocked softly on my door. "We need your help, friend." Would I quick take away Sally, their humongous St. Bernard? "She died sometime in the middle of the night." They didn't want their twins seeing her "like she is."

The Animal Control shack at the edge of town was dark. I honked once. A burly long-haired fellow appeared in the window and pointed at the "Closed for July 4th" sign. I sighed and pointed at Sally, stretched out on the back seat. He came outside to look, sighed back, and gently carried her away.

"You tell Frank and Francine's little ones that Merlin says sorry about Sally. She was a good girl."

Sally was more than just the family pet, it turned out. Merlin said that everyone knew her because each morning, she'd stroll Main Street by herself and nap in Lithia Park.

In her adult years, Sally pulled a mini-sized covered wagon in the July 4th parade. Last year a "Sally for Grand Marshal" petition garnered hundreds of signatures, but Merlin explained she lost out to Bill Highland, the high school principal, "by a hair."

After delivering Sally to Merlin, I found a note on my door from Francine inviting me to join her and the kids in front of the Copper Kitchen, where she'd reserved space for watching the parade. In the city, good luck with that. But here? Here's how. From this town's Chamber of Commerce: "While all space is public and not guaranteed for any individual resident or guest, following our traditional honor system for reserving space would be best done with the use of nontoxic chalk."

Frank couldn't join us. As a volunteer "parade observer," his assignment was keeping an eye out for violators of two (of the 33) "Official Fourth of July Parade Rules and Regulations":

"No squealing tires; burning rubber; visible exhaust; NO WHEELIES!"

"No spurs may be used on any horse."

Up East Main Street marched a color guard of elderly war vets in uniform carrying flags, and shouldering pretend rifles. The Kiwanis, Elks, and Lion's Club marched out of sync in their corny-looking (to me, anyway) hats and vests. Folks applauded politely for The Friends of the Library, Garden Club, Peace Choir, and Amigo Club but whooped and cheered for the "Married Men's Lawn Brigade" on their spiffed-up riding mowers and the police department's three-man bicycle unit performing figure-eights. Not-so-talent-

ed hula and belly dancers seemed out of place for a small-town parade to me but not anyone else. Someone nearby pointed at one. "There's my neighbor! Hi, Marsha!" Satin-sashed beauty pageant contestants waved slow motion-like from flatbed trucks. Gorgeous, jaw-dropping clip-clopping horses passed within feet of us (I'd never stood that close to clip-clopping horses), and clown cowboys broke ranks to let kids pet their mules. Souped-up vintage pickups were reserved for VIPs like the mayor and his wife.

All the while, word spread along the parade route about a farewell-to-Sally gathering at Lithia Park Pond before the "Here-Ye-Here-Ye-Come-One-Come-All!" town picnic. After Frank eulogized Sally, the family sprinkled her ashes into the pond. Some children stood quietly and lit their July 4th sparklers. Some grownups removed their hats. It was lovely.

That done, we headed to the all-you-can-eat corn feed, where you lined up to dunk your cob into a crock of hot melted butter. As darkness came, you lined up again if you wanted to read a portion of the Declaration of Independence on the band shell. A singalong with the community band followed. I figured the grand finale would be our national anthem. It wasn't. Instead, we sang "Happy Birthday to You." After all, this town reasoned, what's the Fourth of July but a big birthday party?

And then, of course, fireworks!

Afterward, I phoned my parents and told them about the Fourth of July in my new home.

61

What a July 4th Swimming Lesson Really Taught Me

Our family's July 4th camping weekend at Devil's Lake a long time ago changed my life.

Dad's friend, Henry Freier, came with us. Henry was macho, spirited, a hugger. And fearless. Nothing and no one frightened him.

The polar opposite of us Schwartz men.

The great outdoors was as alien to me as Neptune. I remember watching in wonder and joyful anticipation while Henry loaded our station wagon with tents, archery equipment, heaps of summer foods, and an aluminum milk crate chock-full with sparklers and cherry bombs.

But when I saw the fishing gear and life preservers and asked him if there would be a lake up there, he said, "Of course," my stomach dropped.

Deep water was my worst fear. I don't know why. What I do recall is how I'd become adept at hiding this fear from friends and family with plausible excuses to avoid water — until that July 4th with Henry.

Earlier that summer, at day camp, I had faked fainting after letting myself get walloped in the head playing dodge ball, and the counselors had excused me (again) from swim class.

The counselors called non-swimmers like me, "shallow-enders." I didn't mind, but Dad was not pleased with that wussy label. Embarrassed, I guess, for both of us.

That's probably why he welcomed Henry's guarantee to purge me of my fear of deep water at Devil's Lake. I was not consulted.

Wedged between my Grandma Ida's Yiddish monologues and my teenage sister's kvetching in the back seat of the Buick, I concocted excuses to avoid Henry.

But I was no match for him. "Let's go," he ordered as he towed me into Devil's Lake. When the water reached my chin, I yelled bloody murder and faked something or other. He ignored that and cradled me firmly in his meaty arms. I remember vividly floating on my back in that humiliating position, terrified he would let go. He didn't, this time.

"Are you a coward, boychik?" Henry asked over and over, holding me in that inglorious position for many minutes until he returned me to the shore because, in his words, it was "time to break bread."

"Tomorrow, you swim or drown," he said. "You choose." I'll never forget those words.

That episode was also when I spotted some faded blue numbers tattooed on Henry's arm: 18091.

At lunch, Henry ate ferociously, as he always did, often with his eyes shut and with no regard to the guttural sounds he was making. A few of us kids secretly called him "Sloppy Poppy." It was mostly about the bread. He devoured it. We didn't understand. It was just bread. That night at bedtime, I asked Mom about Henry — why he "ate like that" and what "those numbers on Henry were for." "Never mind about all that."

"Why?"

"You wouldn't understand. It's none of your business, dear." Seven-year-olds don't acquiesce when told, "You wouldn't understand. It's none of your business, dear."

I went to Grandma Ida. She was sitting in a folding lawn chair drinking her tea near the water. Always the willing storyteller, she'd explain. Not this time.

Instead: "Lozn im aleyn. S 'iz nisht deyn biznes!"

The next morning in Devil's Lake, Henry said, "Take a deep breath," and then he let go.

That night Henry taught us Yiddish folk songs, and we watched the lovely fireworks over Devil's Lake.

In time, of course, I learned that Henry was a Holocaust survivor. But it wasn't until many years later that I came upon a tape-recorded interview with him (you can listen to it on the U.S. Holocaust Memorial Museum website; "Oral History Interview with Henry Freier"), and heard in horrific detail about what Mom and Grandma Ida wouldn't tell me at

Devil's Lake: The ghetto, deportations, Auschwitz, torture, 18091.

And I heard about the bread: "On the train to Grossrosen [from Auschwitz], we didn't have food for three days. When we got there, we got a little bit of soup and a few slices of bread... I finished it almost with one bite. I was praying... give me one hour to live after the war, sleep in a bed with a pillow under my head and have a good meal."

And then, about the American soldiers, liberation, immigration to the U.S., a new life in Minnesota.

At the end of the interview, Henry is asked, "What do you think of Americans and America?"

"The best in the whole world. God bless America!"

On July 4th, I think of Henry and the day he let go of me in Devil's Lake.

Four Words Captured the Sense of Wonder of the Moon Landing

Fifty years ago Saturday, my stoic father, Polish-speaking grandma, normally chatty teenage sister, tearful mother, and I sat speechless on our living room couch as we watched men land and then walked on the moon. We were dumbstruck.

So was Walter Cronkite.

If you're old enough, you might remember what that dean of American journalists said to us viewers when the Eagle landed. Cronkite removed his ubiquitous black-rimmed eyeglasses, rubbed his (probably sweaty) hands together, suppressed a tear or two of his own, smiled like a kid in a candy store, and said:

"Whew, boy!"

And do you remember what he said when Neil Armstrong later stepped onto the moon's surface?

"My golly!"

And then to his broadcast partner, former astronaut Wally Schirra: "Say something, Wally. I'm speechless."

Cronkite, a war correspondent who had flown on bombing raids over Germany, eyewitnessed the Battle of the Bulge, the Nuremberg Trials, and the Tet Offensive, could only express his own amazement and joy this time with childlike exclamations. Yet, those four words perfectly expressed our own thoughts and feelings. Yours too, maybe.

My journalism teacher, Hattie Steinberg, preached that if you want people to care about what you write, "Check your ego at the door." She added: "Less is better."

To drive home her point, she slashed and gutted our pretentious, fancy-schmancy rhetoric mercilessly. Once, she scrawled across (not in the margin of) my "editorial" about the military draft: "What in the world are you saying here? Stop showing off. Just say it!"

Then she handed me her copy of George Orwell's essay, "Politics and the English Language."

"Read this," she said. I did. Orwell rails against fancy-schmancy, pretentious rhetoric. Especially politicians'. Miss Steinberg had underlined two of Orwell's six nonnegotiable rules of writing well:

(ii) Never use a long word where a short one will do.

(iii)If it is possible to cut a word out, always cut it out.

Later into that midsummer night in 1969 and right up through splashdown, the TV networks brought on sci-fi authors such as Ray Bradbury and Kurt Vonnegut and a bunch of scientists and journalists, all of whom opined about the moon and our arrival on it.

Elected officials chimed in, too, of course.

Bradbury: "I'm willing to predict tonight that by the end of the century, our churches will be full again.

Because when we move out into the mystery, when we move out into the loneliness of space, when we begin to discover we really are three billion lonely people on a small world, I think it's going to draw us much closer together."

ABC's Harry Reasoner: "The moon has always had a sort of spooky or evil quality to it. Strange things were always happening by the light of the moon, and most of them were unpleasant."

Eric Severeid, Cronkite's more cynical broadcasting partner: "Of course, the moon now is something different for the whole human race. There's a price for everything. When you got the telephone you lost privacy. When we got the airplane, we lost a sense of travel. When we physically possess the moon, I suppose it will dawn on us ... that spiritually we lose the moon we had for thousands of years. At least in terms of its remoteness, its wonder, and mystery, the romance, and poetry of it. There's a line in Shakespeare's Henry IV... that says, 'methinks 'twere an easy leap to pluck bright honor from the pale-faced moon.' And how any actor henceforth can utter that with a straight face, I don't quite see."

President Richard Nixon: "This is the greatest week in the history of the world since Creation."

But from what I can remember, compared to Cronkite's "Whew boy!" and "My golly!" all those lofty pronouncements seemed like verbal froufrou.

To me, Cronkite had said it all with four words. Miss Steinberg would have been pleased.

With Olympics' Return Come Memories of Unsung Heroes: The Wheelchair Boys

When I need inspiration, I think back to the athletes I met just before the 1984 Olympic Games.

Writing in the New York Times the other day, Lindsay Crouse noted that "we don't have many ways left in our culture to be collectively inspired." The Olympics, she thinks, might be one.

When I need inspiration, I think about the Wheelchair Boys.

I met them a few days before the start of the 1984 Olympic Games in Los Angeles.

Wheelchair Boys is what they called themselves. Four young men who, three times a week, practiced and worked out in the local YMCA swimming pool.

Around that time, I'd finally accepted the sad realization that my pipe dreams of athletic glory, of writing the Great American Novel, of trekking the world, etc., etc., etc., weren't in the cards. Listening to my early middle-aged bellyaching, my wise, elderly neighbor had one day had enough. "Wise up and get a life," he said.

And one morning in July of that year, he drove me to the YMCA and introduced me to the Wheelchair Boys.

They all carried oversized boom boxes on their laps and sported shaved heads. I asked Reggie, their leader, why they shaved their heads. He said, "To swim faster." I made the ignorant mistake of asking him, "What for?" He answered with a cold stare.

Their practice routine was this: They were assisted into the pool one-by-one, each to the tune of a recorded song on his boom box (think baseball players' self-chosen so-called "walk-up" songs but long before that became a popular thing). Paul was first. Van

Halen's "Jump" blasted as two aides sat him on the pool's edge and splashed water onto his frail body. He shuddered, then stuttered in his off-key holler, "Sssstart cccounting!" That was the aides' cue to lift, swing, and, on the count of three, catapult him into the pool.

Paul's teammates hooted and hollered while Paul surfaced slowly, floated facedown for a few seconds in a contorted pose, then began his slow (to us) zigzag course to the shallow end. The boys cheered him wildly with "Go, Paul! Go, Paul! Go, Paul!" and slapped the sides of their wheelchairs.

You knew Paul heard his cheering section because his clawing-like strokes quickened, and he splashed more noisily. When he reached the wall, the boys whooped it up more, especially if he'd bested his previous time.

Next, Mike, hefty and strong in the upper body, was hoisted from his chair into an inner tube to the tune of "Eye of the Tiger." Then he'd power himself through the water as he circumnavigated the pool.

Next came Chuck (Bon Jovi's "Living on a Prayer") and Reggie (Bruce Springsteen's "Born to Run"). They pushed and pulled themselves along the pool walls in a race against the swim pace clock on the wall. All the while, the Wheelchair Boys shouted instructions and encouragement (and occasional off-color taunts), the way all jocks like to do.

That evening after dinner, after other group home residents had dispersed, my wise neighbor, the Wheelchair Boys, and I watched the L.A. Olympics on TV. They talked knowingly about the boycotting Soviets, the first women's marathon, and the prospects for the U.S. men's all-amateur basketball team led by that kid fresh out of college — Michael Jordan.

In time, talk turned to their own stories. They exchanged training tips, boasted about their personal bests, complained of their aching bodies, and shared how they loved to swim.

Two days later, they were back in the pool, racing against the clock just as fiercely as the Olympians in L.A.

I'd come back often to cheer for the Wheelchair Boys.

Heading Off to College Down a Lonesome Road

The waning weeks of summer stir memories from long ago. Before my parents sent this hotshot child off to college, they lectured me on the perils of wearing dirty underwear (Mom) and of bank overdrafts (Dad). But not about, well, you know… homesickness. That didn't enter their minds. Or mine.

It blindsided me at the last minute. Just before hitching a ride with Chuck, a high school acquaintance, in his questionable Plymouth Valiant, friends and I sat around the dining room table — them, not me, predicting PG13 to R-rated antics of my college life to come. "Them" were all I'd ever known: lifelong pals and teammates, all really good at feeding my insatiable ego. I don't ever remember feeling such emptiness before that night.

Then came a quick hug and stiff handshake from Mom and Dad, respectively (their resurrection of, I guess, the timeless kindergarten protocol that when you dropped off your little one on the first day, "Say goodbye. Turn away. Don't look back."), followed by an ominous backfire of that Valiant's engine.

We rocketed into the scary darkness. I was shivering, literally. She quit on us near Santa Rosa, New Mexico. We nursed her into a gas station off Route 66. The mechanic said he would "see what gives in a day or so." We walked down the dusty highway and checked into a dog-eared motel, near just about nothing, to wait. What might have lifted the spirit of others but squelched mine was the televised preseason Vikings game that night. Ever watch a Vikings game in Santa Rosa, New Mexico? Even more gut-wrenching was watching the dreamy "Parkettes," my high school's cheer and dance squad who back then cheered at Viking games — those girls who just weeks ago we lusted for (in our hearts) when they squeezed past us in the cafeteria and classrooms. And now I could only catch a glimpse of them on the flickering black and white TV screen in a sad motel — in Toofaraway, U.S.A.

I told Chuck I wanted to go home. He said, "You? Really?" I was that close to answering, "Yes."

With no guarantees from the skeptical mechanic, we left Santa Rosa with fingers crossed and a lot less money. We crept along the desert highway shoulders and inched up mountains. We coasted down from each summit to cool the engine and save gas (neither of which works). When our gutsy Valiant delivered my deflated body and soul at the dormitory's rear door, I cried for all kinds of reasons.

A dorm attendant handed me a room key, bedding, and toilet paper. My roommate, a local kid, offered a disinterested "Hey. What's up?" and left to spend the evening with his parents. Then a group of manic first-years barged into my room, recruiting for a touch football game on the lawn outside the adjacent girls' dorm. They guaranteed that girls would be watching from their windows.

I followed them. Everyone, except me, seemed so good-looking, so confident, so bursting with joyful anticipation.

That night was the "Welcome Freshmen!" mixer. I stuck close to Chuck until he found a girl he liked. He abandoned me on a bench watching the touch footballers flirt with their adoring new fans.

For the first time, I came to know how it feels to be utterly alone in a crowd.

Then the coup de grace: The next day, my college hosted the U of M Gophers football team. How's that for coincidence? But now, instead of "ski-u-mahing!" in the U's glorious Memorial Stadium on a brisk autumn Saturday afternoon, here I was in a stadium in a desert surrounded by things called "buttes" and 50,000 sweating Gopher haters. I disguised my true allegiance by fake-cheering for the home team and razzing my secret heroes Jim Carter, Walt Bowser, and coach Murray Warmath's other tough guys.

After the Gophers (and I) were humiliated 28-46, I contributed my share of "Oh-man-did-we-crush-those-guys" mockeries with my rowdy dorm-mates, who had already christened themselves the "Dorm Troopers."

Classes started. I wrote a letter to my parents (No such thing as quick-fix texts or Face Timing. Long-distance phone calls? Forget it. Too expensive and unnecessary "except maybe in an emergency," said my dad), planting the idea of leaving at semester break for some bogus excuses about not being "turned on by my classes" and "a boring roommate." In truth, I missed my friends and home. A man of few words, my dad wrote back thusly:

"Kiss the ground you're walking on. Dad"

Translated, he meant: "You're not going anywhere, Hotshot. Grow up."

Somehow, Dad's nonnegotiable edict got the ball rolling. One day, Professor Lightfoot, my observant Freshman Comp professor, caught me staring at a pretty girl. After class, Professor Lightfoot offered to "Miss Foster", my assistance with her "thin" composition. Considering the equally thin piece of dreck I'd written, the professor and I knew I had no business assisting anyone. Nevertheless, I accepted the task because "Miss Foster" was really pretty and because of Professor Lightfoot's charitable wink and a nod.

Not long after, Ray, a Chicago kid who often ate his meals alone, offered me one of his two Santana concert tickets. The concert was great despite menacing looks from some concertgoers, either because Ray wore his ROTC uniform, or because he was black, and I was white, or all three.

We became great friends for a while at just the right time. After that, I abandoned my bogus plans to come home.

Many years later, my wife and I would kiss and hug our daughter goodbye at her dormitory on Move-in Day, turn away, and not look back.

Easier said than done. It hurts to think the odds are good your hotshot kid will feel homesick — if only for a while.

The Fruits of a Lifetime of Labor. Surprise!

When I retired from teaching, on a whim, I signed up to drive for one of those app-based car services. One thing you learn quickly is that with little prompting (like, "So, what do you do?"), most ordinary folks are champing at the bit to talk earnestly (even to a stranger) about their jobs. And if you're lucky, how their jobs or even the jobs of their moms and dads have shaped their lives, for better or worse.

So on this Labor Day, amid the sales, closing up of the cabins, barbecues and the dreading of the next day's start of school, here's a story I was told about one guy's parents' lifetime of plain living and work with, well, a bit of a twist.

Matthew survived the Great Depression up on the Iron Range, because his father taught him how to find work and account for every precious penny that came their way.

Nearby, and at the same time, Matthew's future wife, Lila, and her family had so little that bread-and-ketchup sandwiches were often the main course at dinner. But they worked their farm as best they could and also managed to survive.

Whatever money both families scraped together, they deposited in coffee cans or cigar boxes — not in the town's hanging-by-a-thread savings-and-loan.

Parting with their hard-earned nickels and dimes, quarters, and occasional dollar bills were unthinkable.

When Lila and Matthew married, simplicity, self-preservation, and honorable labor defined their quietly loving and devoted relationship.

Fast-forward many years, to about now. Matthew, having worked steadily and honorably all his life to support the family, was near death. Lila, who soon would live alone in the house they had built by themselves, gathered her grown and now-dispersed children for an announcement she felt was timely and sensible.

Yes, the children remembered that plaid-colored cooler they always used for family picnics. What about it?

And, yes, they remembered that makeshift shower stall she and Matthew had built in their dank basement and which the daughters would hardly use. ("Yuuuuck," they would complain.) What about it?

That's when their mom, according to Pete, who told the tale, led them into the basement. The children watched in bewilderment as Lila removed from the gap between the cement floor of the shower stall and the basement floor like she was removing her homemade pastries from the oven, several cookie sheets upon which rested symmetrically stacked piles of rectangular packages wrapped tightly in tinfoil. All told, there must have been dozens.

79

Back upstairs in the kitchen, their mother also brought out that well-worn cooler, this time filled to the brim with more neatly wrapped packets.

Pete unwrapped a package on the kitchen table.

The children didn't ask questions at first, probably because they were just plain flummoxed at what they saw. But soon, Pete had to ask as the three children unwrapped more of the tinfoil packages: "How much is here, Mom?"

"A lot, by the looks of it, I guess."

"Didn't you and Dad count it?"

"Saw no need to. We had enough to get by."

The children painstakingly counted the bills, all crisp 20s, 50s, and 100s, as if they had come straight from a bank teller's hand into their father's. Which they had.

Turns out that each payday, Matthew cashed his paycheck or, later, his Social Security and pension checks. Then, after paying the bills

— in cash — he took the remainder home, where Lila carefully wrapped and stacked the currency on a cookie sheet or in the cooler. With equal care, Matthew returned the cookie sheet underneath the aforementioned homemade shower stall floor in the basement. "I'm showing you now — just in case," their mother explained. "After we're both gone, we didn't want you selling the house and not knowing.

That wouldn't have been sensible, now would it?" Naturally, her children asked their mom:

"Why didn't you and Dad keep your money in the bank?"

"We didn't want to lose it. We worked hard all our lives for it." Understood. Three hundred and fifty grand is a lot of money.

Lessons in Work — and Life — from the Scrap Yard

Terry, the scrap-yard foreman, looked me over. "Didn't anyone tell you to wear work boots, for Pete's sake?"

I'd shown up on my first day clueless and snarky, wearing white canvas Jack Percell Blue Tips and a button-down shirt — with a pack of wimpy Marlboro Lights in the pocket. All of which elicited guffaws and eye rolls from the lifers, who pegged me as a long-haired hippie, raised-in-suburbia pantywaist English major with an II-S draft deferment and related to Fred, the owner.

All true.

That day I wiped lunch tables, mopped office floors, and pulled weeds. That evening I whined to Dad about wanting a real job, like at a bookstore. Not a scrap yard. He didn't see it that way. "Tomorrow, when you show up, kiss the ground you're walking on. This is a real job."

He further advised me to remove the chip from my shoulder before "those fellas" removed it for me and to "lose those light cigarettes you smoke." He handed me his pack of more manly Old Gold Straights.

"Take these. And don't mouth off. Just do your job."

I got the message. The next morning I came outfitted for work in "the yard." Probably to test my mettle, Terry perched me atop a dump truck to separate mangled aluminum scraps from a heap of newly arrived junk.

I must have passed muster. After four days and three more dump trucks, Terry assigned me to the smelting team. Its task was to melt the aluminum in a fire-belching, ferociously hot, cavernous furnace and pour the molten liquid into foot-long rectangular cast-iron cradles that crawled on what resembled an oversized oval toy train track controlled by an old-fashioned hand-operated lever.

This operation required the coordinated labor of the "stirrer," the "raker," the "spout clearer," and the "flinger," which catapulted each hot ingot from its cradle onto a plywood platform with another hand lever at just the right moment before it returned for a refill.

I learned quickly about this team's daily quest to beat Terry's ingot output quota — despite the glaring absence (in my mind) of bonuses or any other incentives. To my thinking, a lesser amount of aluminum melted meant fewer ingots formed and flung, which meant fewer ingots to stack at the end of the shift, all of which eased the workload and, even more important, reduced the chances of getting badly burned. I'd seen the ugly scars on arms — and faces.

None of this mattered to them. I didn't understand why.

I also learned quickly that critical to the team's quota-busting was winning the daily battle against those unpredictable, impish cradles. They seemed determined to derail and spill their molten aluminum onto the tracks where it would harden on contact.

But Ivan — I swear — stared down those ingrates, daring them in Polish to derail just so he could spring into action and stabilize their wobbly wheels with seconds to spare. Almost always, he saved the day, shouting "Zwyciestwo!" ("Victory!") when he did.

Ivan was probably pushing sixty, worn and always disheveled, compared with the younger bucks around the yard. He was devoutly Catholic and almost became a priest. He often described in tearful, broken English miracles he'd witnessed throughout his lifetime.

Later, when Ivan and I were exiled inexplicably to the graveyard shift for two weeks, he'd build a small fire behind the tool shed and tell me snippets about his life in Poland, his family, and how he — alone — "…sailed to America on the ocean after the Nazis." During break time, I watched his shadow stroll beyond the wall of scrap iron, where he'd stare at the barely visible shoreline across the dark Mississippi River. Returning, he'd say, "OK. Work time." Randy was a Vietnam War vet around my age. He chain-smoked and sang Grand Funk Railroad's "I'm Your Captain" (look up the lyrics if you have the chance) practically all day. Once I asked him, buddy-to-buddy-like, what it was like "over there in 'Nam."

He mumbled something close to "Pretty messed up," which really meant, "Don't ask."

Randy liked to smuggle a six-pack of Grain Belt into the yard and submerge it in the Mississippi to chill. The owners would have fired him for that, but Terry looked the other way. Randy could repair just about any piece of equipment or create ingenious makeshift substitutes on the spot.

And there was Karl, pint-size but amazingly strong. He barely spoke but would high-five Ivan and Randy when we surpassed the quota. Karl ignored me all summer except twice: the time I tried ingratiating myself to him by showing off the aluminum burn scabbing along my forearm. He told me to "piss off." And then, on my last day on the job, when he gave me the upbraiding I needed and had come.

One morning the smelting team punched in, and we found our furnace in rubbles. It had exploded sometime during the night. No one knew how it happened. Terry dispersed us to various jobs around the vast yard. From then on we rarely saw each other.

But on the Friday before the Labor Day weekend, my last day, Terry paired Karl and me to sift through a mountain of scrap containing a mother lode of valuable brass. Tossing pieces blindly over my shoulder, I heard a hollow "thunk." A wallet-sized chunk had nailed Karl square on his head, knocking off his hard hat.

I laughed. "Bull's-eye!"

Karl charged me, grabbed my shirt with both hands, yanked me down to his face, and said exactly this:

"You don't need this job, but I do. I have kids. Do that again, and I'll kill you. Understand?"

I told him I did. I really did.

Then Karl released his vice grip, offered me a cigarette, and we smoked together, silently.

After Labor Day, the fall term began. I ditched my work boots and Old Golds. What remained was that ugly aluminum burn scar on my forearm. I kept it exposed, hoping folks would ask how I got it so I could tell them about my job at the scrap yard.

Later, Uncle Fred told me that he had rebuilt the furnace and that Terry had reunited Ivan, Randy, and Karl.

I envied the guy who took my place.

Lincoln Del Days (and Jobs My Father Got Me)

My father found summer jobs for me without telling me ahead of time. He'd never ask, "How would you like to press sheet metal?" "…melt aluminum scrap?" "…crush cars?"

Instead, he'd say, "You'll be pressing sheet metal this summer."

If (when) I whined, his response was: "Too bad. You're lucky you have a job."

Once, looking to find cushier work, I beat him to the punch. Word had spread about a busboy job at the Lincoln Delicatessen. "The Del" was famous for its one-of-a-kind menu (don't get me started about their triple tootsie, grilled Rueben, grilled Rachel, cheese blintzes, and cream cheese frosting), and for being THE place in our neck of the woods to see and be seen.

Working there would be a lark, I thought.

You didn't fill out an application to bus tables at the Del. What you needed was someone to vouch for you, like a neighborhood yenta or crony of Morrie, the owner. And it helped if Morrie knew (and liked) your father.

An interview with Morrie lasted thirty seconds, whether he hired you or not.

Mine went something like this:

"So you're Arnie Schwartz's kid?" (Uh, yeah.) "You get good marks in school?" (They're OK.)

"Where'd you work last?" (I was a metal sheet presser last summer.)

"How'd you like that?" (Not much. I wasn't good at it.)

"What makes you think you won't screw up this job?" (Pause: I don't know... but I'll try not to...)

Despite my fumfering, Morrie said, "Get to work." He pointed at the petite woman dressed to the nines, standing at the cash register. "Do what Agnes says, or you'll be out on your tuchus."

Not an hour into the job, Mrs. Cornbloom scolded me because her hot pastrami sandwich was "Ayz kalt kalt!" ("freezing cold!"). I pointed out to Mrs. Cornbloom I was "the busboy, not the cook." To Agnes, that sounded smart-alecky, like, "Don't blame me, lady. I'm the busboy, not the cook."

That's when Agnes hustled me down a steep staircase and into a tiny office. "The customer is NEVER wrong..." she began. Then she had me apologize to Mrs. Cornbloom for pooh-poohing her complaint about the freezing-cold pastrami sandwich.

That didn't stop me from trying to make hotshot small talk with other diners. Until Agnes overheard. "Who do you think you are? Some bigshot schtarker? Keep your head down and do your job." But that was nearly impossible when those pretty college girls home for the summer or a local hero like Hubert Humphrey, Sid Hartman, or the Twins' Rod Carew walked into the Del. At times like those, Agnes warned me to stop gawking even before I started. "Let them be," she'd say.

Agnes pulled no punches. Like when she caught you standing still and broadcast from her post at the cash register, "You have nothing to do?" In the world, according to Agnes, there was always one more thing to do. And you'd better do it before she had to tell you to do it.

Fill water glasses with just so much ice. Refill pickled beet and kosher dill pickle appetizer bowls to their brims. Reload the milk and soda dispensers. Scrape shmutz from condiment bottles and laminated menus. Ferret out stray cigarette butts from cracks and crevices in the vinyl booths. Clear, wipe, mop, sweep, restock, repeat.

If you don't think Agnes's demands rivaled those of the hard-boiled foremen of smelters, pressers or car crushers, think again. One morning she said, "Morrie wants to see you in his office."

I assumed I was a soon-to-be-goner, and Agnes was why. Instead, Morrie handed me a blue canvas pouch.

"Take this to our bank. Say it's from me. Bring them a nosh. And don't wreck my car."

89

His gorgeous sky-blue Pontiac Bonneville convertible.

Each afternoon thereafter, Agnes handed me the canvas pouch stuffed with cash, Morrie's car key, and a sack of bagels or pastries. Taking a circuitous route, I'd cruise my neighborhood, wearing the Del's snazzy red busboy jacket, snooty due to my good fortune and thinking with cocksure smugness, "I own this job."

Not quite.

It was a Saturday when Agnes said she needed me to work the next day, my usual day off. But my buddy Malcolm and I had finally persuaded two girls we'd met that summer to tube down the Apple River with us. All through my shift, I pouted and kvetched about how Agnes was ruining my life, hoping she'd hear me and change her mind. She did hear me. But she didn't change her mind. And when she'd heard enough, down, we walked to that tiny office. "You're so fortunate to have a job," she said. "If you want to keep this one, be here tomorrow." She touched my shoulder then left me alone down there to think about it...

Snakes and Martians on Halloween

Here's what happened:

Late into the night of the Great Halloween Blizzard of '91, I snuck a handful of mini Milky Ways from my son's limited Halloween haul and cozied up with hot cocoa, a blanket, and a good mystery.

All was bliss.

Until from the corner of my eye next to my stocking feet, I saw it – glaring, coiled to strike.

I wanted to shout to my braver wife to come downstairs. But I didn't. What if the commotion made it slither into an unknown cranny in our house? Or worse? Then what? I sat very, very still. But the standoff became too much. I dashed to the mudroom.

In there, I dialed 911, described this thing's putrid-green color, and whispered, "What should I do?" 911 suggested I approach it carefully from behind with a pot or pail, "corral it" (She might have said, "capture," I'm not sure] then contact a wildlife removal company.

"Do what?" My cowardice concerning creatures was old news. Once I freaked out at the pigeon cooing on our toilet seat and called 911. And one summer night when my wife was away, thinking it prudent not to bother them again, I got neighbor Tom to extricate a crazed stuck bat from my kitchen sink drain with his fishing net and barbeque tongs.

This was different. In my mind, deadly.

Per 911's instructions, I snuck up from behind with a plastic pail whispering, "Oh, god, oh god, oh, god...) and managed to corral ("capture") the snake. To prevent its attempts to escape, I stacked at least a half dozen encyclopedias on the pail.

Meanwhile, my wife heard the ruckus and came downstairs. I described the snake and how I captured it. She saw me trembling and took charge. "Get me the rubber gloves from the mudroom."

I pleaded with her not to agitate the snake that we needed those emergency pest removal people. She said no way they'd come out tonight, and besides, "Who needs them? Don't worry. I got this." She put on the gloves and lifted the pail.

I hollered. Glaring, it still was and coiled to strike. Then: "Oh," I mumbled.

"Boo!" said my wife, as she tossed the rubber snake back into our son's toy bin and laughed.

So did I. But not right away. Fear, irrational or not, is hard to shake.

Dad wasn't laughing either on a different Halloween night in '38 when he and his twenty-something pals knew that Martians were invading Earth.

When they packed up their moms, dads, little sisters, and brothers to hide out at Manny's cousin's house in Hibbing, where they figured the Martians wouldn't bother.

When my Auntie Dora telephoned him in hysterics, crying, "It's on the radio. Meyn Got. We're going to die."

When they choked up with relief as word spread through their neighborhood that the Orson Welles' "War of the Worlds" radio drama was just that. Martians weren't really invading after all. It was Welles, confessed to America midway into the program, "The Mercury Theatre's own radio version of dressing up in a sheet and jumping out of a bush and saying Boo!"

"You laugh now, but we weren't laughing then," Dad told us.

In his final year, driving him to his ominous medical appointment, we listened to a CD recording of that original radio broadcast. I thought by then we could finally share a much-needed laugh about how long ago he and his buddies were ready to bolt to Hibbing, especially when the "broadcaster" announced:

"The evidence of our eyes lead to the inescapable assumption that those strange beings who landed in the Jersey farmlands tonight are the vanguard of an invading army from the planet Mars....

Something's wriggling out of the shadow like a gray snake.... and it glistens like wet leather.... The eyes are black and gleam like a serpent...."

This time Dad was less bull-headed and laughed a bit. Like before, he admitted to falling "hook line and sinker" but still made no excuses. "We heard on the radio that Martians were invading Earth," he said. "So Martians were invading Earth. We believed it. We were scared to death."

"Really, Dad? C'mon. Of Martians?" "Yes. Martians," he said.

In the spirit of Halloween, I'd tell my students Dad's Martian story, and we'd listen to Welles' "War of the Worlds". Most had a hard time accepting, as one student put it, "... that regular people could be suckered into believing something so fake," and we talked about fake snakes, invading Martians and other things much scarier and real.

Minnesota Winter: I May Not Always Like It, But I'll Always Love It

All bundled up and ready to go: The setting was a park in Savage in January, but it's a classic, almost timeless Minnesota winter scene, of which we just got another reminder.

And you thought winter was over.

Almost, but until then, here are some final thoughts ...

Over the decades, our local meteorologists have honed a certain kind of winter news story into an art form. Any born-and-raised Minnesotan (of a certain age) knows the anticipation of that day-of-days — the "Snow Day."

What an intense moment it was when, with heads pressed against our radio, we listened to the holy grail of our childhood — the list of school closings — read by an exuberant broadcaster who seemed as excited as we were.

"St Agnes School. Closed! St. Anthony Schools. Closed! St. Bonaventure School. Closed! St. Charles Schools. Closed!" "Come on, come on. Just say it," I would whisper.

"St. Cloud Public Schools. Closed!"

And then... "St. Louis Park Schools. Closed!"

Once, after Dad had witnessed my jubilation, I caught him rolling his eyes and sharing a knowing grin with my mother.

Of course, nowadays, the electricity of that moment isn't quite as jolting. The internet spreads the word of school closings more efficiently, though certainly in a less dramatic fashion.

Me? I'll always remember the WCCO broadcaster's voice speaking directly to me, practically ordering my sister and me to stay home and play, play, play!

We're proud of our winter hardiness here in Minnesota. Many of us grew up admiring our neighbors' meticulously groomed sidewalks (and maybe we felt judged by them). We admired how dads manned their shovels dutifully after a snowfall. We admired how adults confronted the elements with fortitude, comradeship, and ingenuity when called upon to extricate their cars from snowbanks, remove ice from their rooftops or thaw out all things that moved.

Before the Metrodome opened in 1982, Minnesota dads would teach the tried-and-true ways of keeping warm during Gophers and Vikings football games at Memorial Stadium and the Met. My dad brought 12-inch stacks of newspaper to place under our feet

— "newspaper is the best insulator," he would say — along with cigars and his flask of what he called "coco."

Layering clothing was a science. Yet Dad never wore a hat before and after '63. I think that's because John F. Kennedy never wore one, and Dad loved JFK.

Our parents taught us how to complain about the cold and snow with a subtle, self-congratulatory air:

"Had to shovel three times to keep up."

"When I was your age, we walked…"

"We slept in our coats and put on more blankets. Kept our heating bill down that way."

Now I watch the shadows of moonlit skaters on our lakes while listening to their muffled voices and the soft scraping of their ice skates. It's certainly more melodic than the cacophony of Minnesota's summer screeching. It seemed the winter sounds travel farther across the still lakes, dissipating into the darkness of who-knows-where. What follows is the welcome silence and solitude that we need more than ever these days.

There was a time when I was mighty pleased to take a hiatus from winter's headaches. I longed for an escape to more tolerable climates, where mentions of dangerous ice, biting winds, fishtailing cars, dead batteries, herniated discs, sandpaper skin, impound lots, and mountains of snow brought only unblinking, ignorant expressions on the natives' faces.

Arizona was the first stop along the way. My most vivid recollection of their "winter" is the humongous Santa Claus cardboard cutouts mounted high on street lamps, sporting cherry red Bermuda shorts with "six-shooters" lodged in huge leather-looking holsters, or pointed toward the cloudless blue sky. It looked like old Sheriff Kringle was shouting "Yahoo!" instead of "To all a good night!" So odd and as far removed from a Minnesota winter as I thought you could get.

Until I moved to Oregon. Imagine December fog settling in almost every day, dispiriting clouds hanging low, dampness enveloping the dull green landscape.

One winter, a rare snowfall dusted the landscape, a pretty lame attempt at winter if you ask me. I was alone at the time and actually became teary-eyed. It made me ache for a Minnesota winter, flaws and all.

Next up, Brooklyn, N.Y. If you haven't experienced a Brooklyn winter, I assure you they are very ornery. Sure, moments of winter splendor would surprise us. When it snowed in Brooklyn, you had a four-hour window in which to frolic in a quasi-winter wonderland before its transformation into a world of grime and slush. That did it for me.

Full circle back to Minnesota. The prodigal son returned, more appreciative than ever of winter's lovely side.

But I found winter was less welcoming than expected, my older self less willing and able to enjoy and tolerate the frigid temps. Shoveling and even snow-blowing were now risky activities, not the invigorating workouts they once had been.

The art of layering cotton, fleece, and wool became less effective in easing my stiff joints. Winter seemed more in line with Robert Byrne's idea that "Winter is Nature's way of saying, 'Up yours.'"

The coup de grace was the year I picked to return: 1991. Remember the Halloween Blizzard?

I still watch with bemusement the recycled segments on TV news about how to avoid frostbite, shoveling safely, or how to dress the kids "for the bus stop."

I admit to feeling a kind of misplaced sense of victory when "we" break the record for snowfall or low temperature. I admit to just a bit of schadenfreude when a TV reporter snares a car owner for a sound-bite interview at the impound lot after a snow emergency. And I admit, I still tune in to WCCO on wintry mornings with a weird hope that my alma mater will be among the list of school closings. I'm thrilled when it's announced and bummed when it isn't.

Minnesota Winter is in my blood. It's who I am. I may not always like it, but I'll always love it — and need it.

An Almost Meatless Thanksgiving

"Nothing revives the past so completely as a smell once associated with it."

Vladimir Nabokov

I recently came upon a cooking supplement in the New York Times (Sidesgiving, November 14th) offering thirty recipes to help create "...a Thanksgiving meal that's beautiful, lavish and vegetarian..." Dishes like: Cheesy Hasselback Potato Gratin; Hashed Brussels sprouts with Lemon; Pan-Griddled Sweet Potatoes With Miso-Ginger Sauce; and Creamed Greens Potpie.

Sounds delicious. But "Forget the turkey"? as the supplement suggests? I'm here to tell you that even now, forty-four years since my last taste of it, just one whiff of a buttered and seasoned roast turkey makes my mouth water accompanied by crystal clear memories of Thanksgiving pasts.

How easy I'm able to recall them. Especially awakening to the perfect aroma of "your mother's turkey," as Dad would call it, already roasting in "Mom's oven". Still, in my pajamas, she'd hand me a sliver of dark meat, my favorite. "How's this?" she'd tease.

And all day, our small home was filled with an intoxicating aroma I still can't describe.

We loved meat. Mostly because Dad demanded we have meat at every dinner and because Mom was the devoted keeper of sacrosanct handwritten family recipes. So we grew up on her lamb chops, brisket, cow's tongue, Saturday Steak Night, heaps of cured ('hard") Hebrew National salami sandwiches in front of the TV

on Viking game Sundays, and of course for an anytime nosh, her chopped liver, flavored with Old-World piquant gribenes, chicken schmaltz, spicy herbs, and sweet onions, all of which were catalysts for Dickens-like (and sometimes bawdy) stories about our still-living and long-gone relatives.

But we all agreed that Mom's piece de resistance was her Thanksgiving turkey. I once boasted to the kids on the playground that my mother's turkey tasted and smelled best of all, and my friend Hershel and I got into a nasty shoving match about that. After Principal Halverson called home to report the incident, Mom hugged me.

Had I recalled her loving hug one particular Thanksgiving many years later, I could have saved my family a long weekend of heartache:

I'd recently moved to a mountainous spot out West. Unbeknownst to me, the town was a leftover haven for 1960s hippies and a likely place to "find yourself," as we said back then. Aching to assimilate, I transformed (or disguised) myself from a born-and-raised mid-western suburbanite into a lover of all things nature and, with that, a rejecter of all-things meat.

By Thanksgiving time, I was excited to display the newest me to family and friends back home. Sporting my first beard, bandana, patched bell-bottoms, and Birkenstocks (with white socks no less), I assumed my parents and relatives would be impressed. Especially when I announced, "And also, I don't eat meat."

Blinded by youthful self-absorption, I might as well have announced my conversion to another religion or no religion.

You should have seen the expression on Mom's face. Remember the film "Saturday Night Fever" and Tony Manero's mother's

heartache and feeling of betrayal when Tony's older brother Frank, Jr. announces to the family he's quitting the priesthood? Like that. Maybe worse.

On Thanksgiving, I was coming out as a vegetarian. "Who put you up to this?" (No one.)

"Mark my words. You'll eat my turkey." (No, Ma. I won't.")

"Arnold, Talk sense to him."

Out of Mom's earshot, Dad said something like, "Would it have hurt you to wait until after Thanksgiving? How can someone who went to college be so dumb."

For the next couple of days, Mom pulled out all the stops to break me. I avoided her sad, bloodshot eyes and somehow fended off the seductive aromas of her sizzling bacon, brisket, corned beef hash, lamb chops, and chopped liver. But, as it turned out, not her turkey.

The poet Rudyard Kipling once said, "Smells are surer than sights and sounds to make your heartstrings crack." Mine did. In short, on Thanksgiving morning, I awakened to the aroma of "your mother's turkey". That evening, as was our tradition, we toasted health, togetherness, and grateful for. Then, as was her custom, Mom dimmed the dining room lights and placed her turkey on the candlelit table. We oohed and aahed and lavished her with compliments. Dad carved hefty pieces for everyone, including for me, without asking.

My vegetarian ways could wait.

"You've made your mother happy. Maybe you're not so dumb after all," he announced.

For the rest of the weekend, we watched football and ate leftovers.

Several days after I'd returned to my new home out West, I received a large package. A note read "Just in case. Love, Mom." She'd packed inside Folger's coffee cans

103

chopped liver, a thick kosher salami and of course, more turkey leftovers.

Thanksgiving Far From Home

I was stranded at my college one Thanksgiving because I was a know-it-all freshman who assured his parents, "I'll book my own flight." By the time I got around to trying, the flights were full. Not one seat. When I broke the news, Mom wept into the phone, and Dad hauled out his "It serves you right" speech, but he sounded more disappointed than angry.

Dreading being alone, I practically begged Nurse Guevara for a double shift at my part-time orderly job at the Kivel Nursing Home. She agreed.

On Thanksgiving morning, before my first shift, I sat in the dormitory commons room with one other marooned kid. He said he roomed on the fifth floor, but he was the only one up there. Everyone else had gone home.

The Minnesota Vikings-Detroit Lions game came on television. It was hard for me to watch it with a random companion, knowing my living room back home was packed with family, friends, and relatives at the same time. No doubt they were doing handsprings when Jim Marshall intercepted that pass and tossed a no-look lateral to Alan Page, who scored the touchdown in a snowstorm.

Watching that in real-time choked me up. Not the touchdown. The snowstorm. I ached to inhale that wintry Minnesota air instead of the alien aroma of Phoenix's stockyards.

I missed dressing for cold weather. I missed the winter quiet in the nighttime. I missed home.

Later that day, I punched in early for my first shift and headed straight to Mr. Ryan's room.

Everyone adored Timothy Ryan. At 90-something, he was still handsome and gregarious, a real charmer. He could make the raunchy ditties he sang in his melodic Irish brogue sound like love songs. He often spoke about a girl who, way-back-when, was the love of his life. Her name was Claire, and he kept her picture in his breast pocket.

Mr. Ryan's hands and legs were gnarled from arthritis and practically useless. And he was blind.

On this night, Nurse Guevara informed me, "You're on your own with Mr. Ryan tonight." Leaving nothing to chance (I was still an "orderly-in-training"), she handed me a notecard.

As I recall, she had written these reminders:

1) Wash hands and face, 2) brush teeth, 3) comb hair, 4) urinal, 5) pajamas, 6) into bed, 7) turn off lights, 8) whiskey.

About the time I figured Dad was carving "your mother's turkey", as he liked to call it, I was tending to Mr. Ryan and doing fine, I thought.

When at last I transferred him to his bed and turned off the lights, Mr. Ryan offered his customary reminder: "You won't be forgetting our drink now, will ya."

Mr. Ryan was allowed a half shot of whiskey at bedtime. Each night the orderly brought out a bottle and two shot glasses from a cabinet — two shot glasses because Mr. Ryan wouldn't drink alone. He filled Mr. Ryan's shot glass halfway and pretended to

pour one for himself. Then Mr. Ryan and the orderly toasted each other with a "Here's to ya," clinked glasses, and Mr. Ryan downed his shot with one swallow. Just like that, he was asleep.

That's just how it happened on this night with my first solo attempt. It was lovely.

Most late nights in a nursing home are uneventful. Not this one.

With no warning, Mr. Ryan started hollering furious gibberish and curses. When I got to his bedside, he hooked one arm around mine and flung wild swings in my direction with the other.

I'd forgotten step 4.

Nurse Guevara came to my rescue. She took charge, expertly turning Mr. Ryan side to side with one hand while I struggled to remove and replace his wet bedding and pajamas. That done, she said something like, "I'll leave you to sort things out," and left the room.

Mr. Ryan lay still. I was shaking, near tears. "Mr. Ryan, I'm sorry…" He stopped me and found my hand.

"No need for that. You won't be forgetting our drink now, will ya?" After Mr. Ryan fell asleep again, I sat next to him, still. Not for his sake. For mine.

When I returned to my dormitory in the morning, I tracked down the kid from the fifth floor. I think we watched more football, tossed a Frisbee around, and listened to records. I don't remember much about him except that he was from Indiana and thought Led Zeppelin was the greatest rock 'n' roll band ever.

Later that night, I called my parents. I told them all about my Thanksgiving with the kid from the fifth floor and Mr. Ryan.

To This Village Person, My Very Deepest Thanks

This week at Thanksgiving dinner, when it's my turn, I'll express gratitude for many things — family, friends, the food on the table, a certain magnificent doctor, the Social Security check, a home.

That said, it will be high time I thank a guy named Randy Jones. You might know who I mean. He's the "cowboy" of The Village People.

In the late 1970s, our disco-crazy country was singing and dancing to their megahit, "YMCA".

It's fun to stay at the Y... MCA,

It's fun to stay at the Y... MCA-A...

Randy Jones was one of those people who appear and disappear in your life in a flash but manage to change everything. We've all had at least one, I think.

Jones changed my world one Thanksgiving a long time ago. What happened was this:

Earlier that year, I'd met a charming, classy Manhattanite at a wedding I crashed (another story) here in Minneapolis. We small-talked, flirted, and into autumn exchanged schmaltzy letters and poetry about our stars aligning (no cellphones or e-mail back then).

The girl, as I thought of her, suggested I come to New York for Thanksgiving. I'd never been to New York. New

York scared me. New York was about blackouts, Mafia hits, grimy subways, getting lost. I balked.

But Billie Greenberg, my transplanted roommate, Brooklyn-born-and-bred, rolled his eyes New York-style:

"What the matter with you? It's New York City. And there's a girl. Go."

I went. To pay for the plane ticket, I sold the guitar I had no intention of learning to play but schlepped around town anyway because I thought it looked good. When you're young and trying out who you think you want to be, you do things like that.

The girl met me at the arrival gate (back then, you could do that) and drove us expertly into Manhattan. First stop, Macy's Thanksgiving Day Parade. She found us a great viewing site on top of the stone wall that stretched along Central Park West. We held tightly to each other for balance, warmth, and the titillation that until then had been expressed only in those sappy letters.

We heard the Village People before we saw them. Then, decked out in their macho pizazz, there they were — the cowboy, the helmeted cop, the Native American chief, the leather-clad biker, the hard-hatted construction worker — singing (well, lip-syncing), shimmying and high-stepping disco style on a float with a rainbow-colored arch:

Young man... there's no need to feel down,

110

I said, young man... pick yourself off the ground,

I said, young man... 'cause you're in a new town...

The float stopped smack-dab in front of us. I pretended indifference. Then Randy Jones, the cowboy, spotted the girl and me perched on that wall behind the crowd. I know he pointed and smiled broadly at us because, when he did, parade watchers followed his finger to the oddly matched country boy wannabe wearing overalls, flannel, and Birkenstocks and the stylish New Yorker, arm-in-arm.

When The Village People started performing "YMCA" yet again, kids, parents, bell-bottomed teens, even geezers around us sang along happily and mimicked that all-the-rage arm choreography spelling the letters Y — M — C — A.

A closeted lover of disco music, I abstained. Disco didn't jive with overalls, flannel, and Birkenstocks.

Right then, spontaneously, the girl and I shared the first of what's become 40 years of kisses. I remember how sure I was The Village People cowboy had given us the green light with his point and a smile:

"Go on. What are you two waiting for?"

The remainder of our weekend together was lovely (except for her family's bafflement during Thanksgiving dinner about this outlander from "Minndianapolis"). The girl led me by the hand around New York: walks through Central Park, lunch at Carnegie Deli, ice skating under the Christmas

111

tree at Rockefeller Center, the mind-blowing panoramic view of the city at sunset from the observation deck of the World Trade Center...

Alas, Sunday came. A city-savvy (yet sentimental) taxi driver saw the girl and me embracing on a busy street corner next to my suitcase. On my lonely ride to the airport, he said he'd driven twice around the block to give us more time to say goodbye. Then he declared — because New York taxi drivers know everything: "You'll see her again."

He was right.

I've often pictured the girl and me standing on that stone wall on that Thanksgiving morning. Was it a random hit among a lifetime of many more misses when The Village People float stopped in front of us? Dumb luck? Divine intervention? Fate? Forrest Gump's mother called it "destiny." Mine called it "bashert." Yiddish for "it was meant to be."

Who knows?

I only know that at Thanksgiving dinner, I'll count my blessings and thank my lucky stars — along with, this time, Randy Jones of The Village People — for the charming and classy New York girl still sitting next to me.

Everyday Thanks

I'm thankful for...

My next-door neighbor who tolerates my barking dog.

Newspapers that can and will print both sides of the issues.

Surgeons' know-how and courage.

Firefighters' and cops' know-how and courage.

Libraries.

People who are willing to do what I haven't done — tend to the homeless face-to-face.

Writers who can make me laugh and cry.

The anonymous person who snow blows my sidewalk.

Teachers who really know their subject and care about kids.

Drivers who don't hit the gas pedal when the light is yellow.

The cashier at the grocery store, who warns me with a serious smile to stop buying chocolate so often.

Our newspaper delivery person, who leaves the paper within inches of our front door — every time.

How the change of seasons around here reminds us that life offers the chance at "do-overs".

BBC radio in the middle of the night when I can't sleep.

Columnists who can put into words what I can't express myself.

That joke about the snail someone told me that I laugh over whenever I think about it.

Miss Mengelkoch, my eighth-grade teacher, who made us memorize and recite the "Queen Mab" speech from Shakespeare's "Romeo and Juliet".

Watching and listening to really old people laugh with each other.

A Billion Noels? This Minnesota Jew Revels in Christmas Song

Upon reading "Enough with the Christmas songs", Wendy Jacobson, Star Tribune, December 8th, 2016), I got to thinking.

Like the "annoyed" author of that commentary, I'm Jewish. But this Jew loves Christmas music. Last night, when Christmas Eve and the beginning of Hanukkah met up for the first time since 1959, a local radio station that offers 24/7 caroling joyfully accompanied our family's gift-gifting, latke-eating, menorah-lighting festivities. Christmas songs sung by Burl, Nat, Andy, Petula, Elvis, Ol' Blue Eyes, Brenda, Bing, Bruce, and even Bobby (Dylan/Zimmerman) were happily welcomed into our home — for the "billionth" time.

Here's why:

When I was a little guy, Principal Blunt scared the daylights out of me. In my mind, she was the doppelgänger of Dorothy's (Judy Garland's) green-skinned, red-tongued, ugly-black-shoe-wearing Wicked Witch of the West, both of whom starred in my recurring nightmares. Nevertheless, it turns out Principal Blunt is most responsible for my love of the music of Christmas.

More about Principal Blunt later.

As soon as Christmas decorations appeared in our classroom, our clan of second-graders obsessed with predicting the surprises our teacher Mrs. Feldman (yes, that's right — Mrs. Feldman), was dreaming up for that year's class Christmas party. (Yes, we called it the "Christmas party.")

That morning Darnell Worm and I bounded to school through deep snow way too early. As luck or destiny would have it, we came upon Mrs. Feldman unloading a slew of grocery bags from her pea (We called it "pee") green DeSoto. She must have enjoyed toying with our fixation on those packages and matter-of-factly asked us to schlep them into the classroom and then shooed us outside.

I imagine we anguished through arithmetic, reading, even recess until our joyful anticipation reached its apex with Mrs. Feldman's edict to "Clear your desks, fold your hands and sit up straight." Back then, I was vying for the coveted Class Posture King award, so no living being sat more erect than I did; I figured it increased the chances of Mrs. Feldman calling on me to help her get the party started.

I was right.

From under her desk, she presented the class "music box." Out of its depths came our favorite means of diversion from everything boring: rhythm sticks, maracas, and kazoos! My preposterous-looking but obsessive resolve to "sit up straight" paid off because she picked me to distribute the

116

instruments (and hoard one of the coveted kazoos for myself).

The joy we had making music! Under Mrs. Feldman's direction, we pounded, shook, blew, and sang "Deck the Halls", "Good King Wenceslas", "God Rest Ye Merry, Gentlemen" and, of course, "Santa Claus is Coming to Town". Mrs. Feldman also had one of the other Jewish kids teach the class how to sing "The Dreidel Song", too.

After the music-making, Mrs. Feldman served us red bug juice in tiny paper cups, candy canes, cupcakes, and homemade butter cookies with red-and-green candy sprinkles and blue-and-white ones, too. She also prepared a colorful plate of treats "for Santa", which Darnell noted was pretty dumb because it was the middle of the day.

Sometime during that sugary feast, we heard Principal Blunt's sinister shoes approaching. You could always hear her shoes echoing in the hallway, souring our stomachs with acidic fear. Which one of us would she snatch this time? When she appeared in the doorway in her usual uncompromising black dress, rimless eyeglasses, and those god-awful pitch-black shoes, we sat waiting in stone-cold silence.

But for once, there was no curt summons for one of us to "follow me." Principal Blunt peered into our classroom, spoke briefly but surreptitiously with Mrs. Feldman, and left.

117

Clueless about her mysterious coming and going, we assumed it was about our raucous celebrating. Too loud? Too wild? Too messy? With Principal Blunt, you erred on the side of caution, so it took little urging from Mrs. Feldman for us to scrub our desktops and pick up "every bit of trash from the floor around [our] desks." Good timing, because soon after, once again came the ominous staccato rat-a-tat-tats of "Youknowwho's" shoes on the shellacked wooden hallway floor.

A day that had begun with such promise would not end well. Or so we thought.

What happened, suddenly and unexpectedly, was the appearance of Santa — herself — adorned in a makeshift blazing red felt coat and hat, fluffy-white (cotton ball) beard, and black boots. Well, not exactly boots. They were those sinister black shoes, but this time colorized with huge — really huge — red crepe-paper bows.

We sang a few more Christmas songs with the disguised Principal Blunt (which seemed extraordinary to me). Mrs. Feldman gave her the plate of cookies, and the party was over.

I don't remember if Principal Blunt wished us "Merry Christmas" and a "Happy Hanukkah," too. But for sure, she added to our merriment and happiness and gifted us with a memory for the ages.

Since then, on Christmas Eve and Hanukkah, we've cherished Nat's exquisite "The Christmas Song (Chestnuts Roasting on an Open Fire)," Brenda's "Rockin' Around the Christmas Tree" and Bing's "I'll Be Home for Christmas" a "billion" perfect times — all of them a joyful accompaniment to the dreidels, latkes, gelt and a story about how a long time ago we sang a cappella with Santa, aka Principal Blunt. They grace our home with good cheer, comforting melodies, and, maybe most important of all, a brief respite from a lot of, well, unpleasant things.

As the song says: "For we need a little Christmas/ Right this very minute…"

An Introduction to Hanukkah at the Christmas Pageant

In early December of the year, Dad relocated our family to a small town far north of the Twin Cities. Mr. Hahn, the school principal, rang our doorbell. I answered the door and nearly peed my pants when I saw him standing on the step. "Are your parents at home, young man?" he asked.

They were. He said to them that since I was "the only Jewish child" (or "the first Jewish child," I can't recall) at Lewis and Clark Elementary School, I would be "explaining your holiday" at the upcoming school Christmas pageant. He said he believed students needed to "learn about religions like yours."

Principal Hahn was not a man you — kids nor parents — trifled with. Mine immediately agreed. I was not consulted.

Here's what happened:

Anyone could tell the annual Christmas pageant was a big deal at Lewis and Clark Elementary School. Working fathers left work in the middle of the day and showed up wearing suits and ties and sat with dressed-up mothers and grandparents in folding chairs roped off with a sign on each one, "reserved for an adult guest."

Kids didn't need reminding to sit up straight and cross-legged on the floor with hands folded in their laps. No outstretched legs or sitting up on your knees, or leaning back on your elbows were permitted. And, via the intercom the day before, Mr. Hahn had warned us he wouldn't tolerate "tomfoolery." I'd never heard that word where I'd come from and had to ask what it meant.

The lights in the gym dimmed. The Lewis and Clark Elementary School choir (including me) entered from behind a makeshift curtain wearing choir robes our mothers had been instructed to fashion from (only white) bedsheets and ridiculously oversized bows made from red butcher paper. We stood stoically on risers, unlike during the rehearsals when we had had a great time discreetly jabbing each other and causing the other to teeter and hopefully fall off.

Not now. This was serious business.

We sang "O Come, All Ye Faithful" as older students walked in unison into the gym. A spotlight guided them down the center aisle. Some carried nativity scene props — plastic palm trees, the manger, some hay, stuffed farm animals, and someone's pet donkey — ahead of the bearded wise men, some kindergarten angels, and finally Joseph and Mary with the baby Jesus. When all were in place on the stage, the Nativity was re-enacted. When that was over, our choir sang "Silent Night," the lyrics of which (along with several other songs of Christmas) I was required to memorize.

Now came my turn. The school custodian carried out a small table in one hand and my family's plastic electric menorah in the other and plugged it in. Mr. Hahn explained that "fourth-grader Richard Schwartz" would now present a holiday his family celebrates called "Cha-nu-ka." That was the first time I'd heard Hanukkah pronounced "CHA-nu-ka." Where I came from, the "Ha" in "Hanukkah" had that guttural Old World Yiddish sound.

I began with a reading of the Hanukkah story. I remember little about the reading except for my monotone delivery, the occasional braying of the donkey still on stage, and the sprinkling of suppressed giggles. Next, I twisted each bulb to "light" the menorah (no flames in the gymnasium were allowed). I remember feeling a nauseating wave of adolescent dread that despite Mr. Hahn's stern warning, kids would laugh anyway at my chanting of the Hanukkah blessing in Hebrew, which up to then was as familiar to me as English but now seemed terribly alien:

"Baruch Atah Adonai Eloheinu Melech Haolam, Asher Kidshanu B'mitzvotav V'tzivanu L'hadlik Ner Shel Hanukka."

But they didn't. The gym was silent like they had never heard anything like this.

After the pageant, kids asked me some inevitable questions: "What's it like to be a Jewish?" "How'd you learn to talk like that?" "But you still have Christmas, don't ya?"

The following Sunday, the local newspaper ran a photograph of me standing behind the lighted menorah. (Oddly, it appeared in the paper's "Women Section.") The caption reads, "Hanukkah, a Jewish festival of lights, which is celebrated this time of year, was explained by Richard Schwartz."

That photograph is in front of me as I write this. In the background, kids in the choir are staring my way. The donkey is off to the right, but you can't see it. The gym is dark except for the spotlight on me. I just wish I knew what that young boy in the photograph who had just sung "Silent Night" by heart and moments after had chanted a Hanukkah blessing was thinking.

I do know that after the Lewis and Clark Elementary School Christmas Pageant, Principal Hahn shook my hand and said, "Thank you, young man."

For Jewish Teen, Christmas at Patty's was a Foreign but Magical Land

I don't celebrate Christmas, per se, but I'm thankful this happened once, even if it was a long time ago …

A stranger in a strange land is how I felt standing at Patty's doorstep on Christmas Eve.

"You must be Patty's friend from school," her mom said. I balked. "It's all right. Come in." She took my coat and disappeared with it. Their house was filled with light and aromas I didn't know existed. Every Hanukkah, my house was permeated with the

eye-watering smells of spiced-up knishes, kishkah, kreplach, broiled chicken livers, and mounds of greasy garlic, onion, and potato latkes. And the Hanukkah menorah we dutifully lit each night was lovely, even moving.

But here! Here were exotic scents of a fireplace fire, pine, cinnamon, and an oven roasting something I was sure I'd never eaten, along with candles glowing in each window and Christmas lights strung just about everywhere.

Patty seemed nervous when she appeared from the staircase. It must have been awkward for her to stand in her own home on

Christmas Eve with this Jewish boy, who after band class just a day or so before Christmas vacation (yes, that's what it was called) had asked her to wear his ring.

"But I'm going to take it off when I play clarinet," she stipulated. That night, to keep the ring from slipping off her finger, she wreathed it with pink yarn.

I gripped my gift for her inside a thin rectangular Dayton's box. I'd picked out a scarf myself. It was gray, blue, and white with twisted tassels. My sister said it looked like my tallis, my prayer shawl, adding the tease that I'd better not mix them up, considering I was gifting my "cute little Christian girlfriend."

My Old World grandmother nearly plotzed when she heard the words "Christian" and "girlfriend."

"Meyn Gat! A shiksa?!" she wailed.

My New World mom stepped in. "Mama, tuh nischt shrayen. Patty es a zeyer sheyn meydl. Dickie leyx ir," she said.

I understood just enough Yiddish to know. Mom had come to my defense. She told Dad to drive me to Patty's house so I could deliver my gift.

He did. At the curb, he lectured me about remembering to wish Patty and her parents a "Merry Christmas." He was adamant.

125

I wish I could remember more of what Patty and I said to each other in her hallway. But after some bumbling moments, she told me to take off my shoes and follow her into the living room. In there was the whitest carpeting I'd ever seen, a piano, and in a corner, their exquisitely decorated, ceiling-high Christmas tree. I'd never been so close to one, and I know I got teary.

Patty sat me on the piano bench, disappeared, then returned with cocoa and a plate of Christmas-looking cookies. "I made these," she said. We nibbled and sipped next to that dazzling tree until her mom gently called from the kitchen something like, "Patty, it's time for your friend to go home now."

"See you at school," I must have said. "Here."

And I self-consciously handed over the Dayton's box. Mom had no Christmas wrapping at home, but she found a stray ribbon to tape on it. It looked like a castaway ragamuffin, dull as dishwater compared to those treasures under the tree. I urged Patty to open it right then so to get rid of that embarrassing box before her family saw it. But she placed it with the other presents.

"It's all right. Don't worry," I know she said to me. Considering the ring with pink yarn and all, I'd hoped we could kiss quickly — but her mom appeared with my coat and Patty's cookies wrapped in waxed paper.

Dad was dutifully waiting with the motor running. He immediately asked if I'd remembered to wish Patty and her family a Merry Christmas. I said yeah.

"Good. Let's go home. Dinner's waiting."

Which was a big deal because we knew Mom had prepared our family's traditional "Christmas Eve meal" — in those days, there wasn't much else for Jews to do on that night but hunker down at home — matzo ball soup, chopped liver, brisket, kasha and carrot cake with white icing.

This time Mom added Patty's Christmas cookies, despite my grandmother's slow burn. She refused to eat one. "Dreck!" she hissed under her breath. The rest of us ate them all.

By the time school resumed, Patty had replaced the pink yarn on my ring with colors that matched her new scarf. She wore the ring for a couple of weeks until who knew what happened and she gave it back.

At the end of the school year, our family moved a mile or two to an adjacent suburb. In the hearts and minds of 13-year-olds, it was akin to a faraway land. We never saw each other again except once. A few years later, Patty was sitting in the visitor bleachers at our high schools' basketball game. I waved. She waved back. That was it.

Still, I cherish the memory of the short-but-sweet Christmas Eve I spent with Patty a long time ago. It seems like yesterday.

A Magical Bit of Cheer at 30,000 Feet

We just want to get home.

Our plane's crew is as disappointed as we are. We're just all very tired, a certainty that time is running out and the helplessness have smothered what is left of our holiday spirit.

We just want to be home.

We reach the Rockies. Even in the blackness, or because of it, the snow-packed peaks below us are gorgeous. But they make us feel so small, so alone, so unimportant. That something so achingly beautiful can create such angst is physically painful.

Then the silence is broken. We hear the static of the onboard PA system. What now?

The flight attendant's voice cuts in and out, but we can hear fragments:

"Folks, can I please have your attention." Phrases like "interrupted beverage service", "potential bumpiness as we cross the Rockies" and "remain seated with your seat belts securely fastened" are clear enough.

So is the ominous announcement that she will provide us with the latest connecting flight changes "when they become available."

What follows even a seasoned traveler finds unnerving: "Folks, this is the captain. At this time, we have an additional important message, so please listen carefully."

The silence in the cabin deepens. We just want to be on the ground — and home.

I don't celebrate Christmas. But I've lived my life surrounded by it and have come to enjoy, vicariously, its lovely message of peace, comfort, and hope. I am happy when it snows on Christmas Eve and disappointed when it doesn't. I enjoy the joyful commotion of the season and its peacefulness, as well.

The onboard PA shuts off, then turns on again. A moment later, I look at the now-awake passenger to my right and the staring lady to my left, who is touching my shoulder gently. Both are smiling, just a little.

The cabin remains as quiet as before, but it's a different quiet now. That's because someone — we'll never know who — accompanied only by the muffled sound of the jet engines is singing "I'm Dreaming of a White Christmas."

Soon we land. We are closer to home.

It's Still a Wonderful Life

I don't celebrate Christmas per se. But that doesn't mean I haven't watched "It's a Wonderful Life," the mother of all Christmas movies, as many times as you have.

The first time came after an endless nightmare flight over the Great Plains and the Rocky Mountains in a blizzard. When the apologetic pilot landed his plane — don't ask me how — and wished his shaken passengers a Merry Christmas, I dragged myself from the airport to a dingy downtown bus terminal where I caught the last departure by a hair for home, still another three hours away.

I had no headphones to tune out the sad silence on the bus, probably caused by an array of despairing and desperate scenarios that led my fellow passengers to that pilgrimage at that hour — a Trailways bus creeping along an icy highway at midnight on Christmas Eve.

Finally home, drained and alone, I collapsed on the couch, where I came upon a dead-of-night showing of "It's a Wonderful Life." Even before those quirky Bedford Falls townsfolk toasted their humble hero, George Bailey, as "the richest man in town" and sang "Auld Lang Syne" even before Clarence Odbody, Angel Second

Class earned his wings for restoring George's will to live — I was a dewy-eyed mess.

Had the ugly events of my travels not led to that moment, I probably would have passed over a Star Tribune commentary (http://bit. ly/RonMeador) about the film a few years later. I still have it. Each year around Christmas (and Hanukkah for me), I reread it. In years past, I'd share it with my students.

Some of the young curmudgeons pooh-poohed the film as old-fashioned drivel "that my parents make us watch." But the commentary's author at first felt the same way, and I have a hunch even my students were secretly moved by his elegant description of the at once lovely and chilling lessons he finally learned from it.

My classes found much to talk about. We laughed at some of the film's archaic (to them) cartoonishness. But tears were shed, too. If I were still teaching, I'd especially make them read it this year. The column was titled, "Like George Bailey, he's been to the bridge" (December 19th, 1996).

Even if you've seen the movie just once (which is unlikely), I'll bet you remember "the bridge."

That's where George Bailey almost takes his own life when the Scrooge-like Mr. Potter frames him for misappropriating $8,000 from the savings and loan Bailey runs. Hope was gone, and without help (he thinks), George decides (after Potter plants the seed) that he's "worth more dead than alive."

And then the bridge.

Star Tribune Editorial writer Ron Meador wrote about how he had ended up in the same place, emotionally. "It wasn't because of wanting to die, particularly ... because of a death or divorce, or a lost love or upended career, although I've known all those dark passages and some others." He explained how, like George Bailey, he was "propelled to the bridge by a swirl of events that might have been manageable in other circumstances, but now combined to overwhelm me."

It's the "might have been manageable in other circumstances" that make this piece seem especially poignant now.

Meador went on to tell his readers: "It would have been embarrassing and painful to say these things in public if I did not know how common this experience is."

He said coming to know that enabled him to talk about his personal hardships with others, to be less afraid now, and to realize that "...however miserable and worthless you may feel, you always have a hand to extend to another."

And when you do, "You realize that it's a pretty good life — even, from time to time, a wonderful life."

I'll never forget how, in spite of or because of (who can know?) my bleak homebound journey many Christmas Eves ago, I happened upon for the first of many times thereafter, the comfort and joy of "It's a Wonderful Life."

Part 2

Teachers and Students

Teaching: Oh! The Humanity!

In June, I will retire from teaching. Here are some moments from those 41 years. Not the "big moments," necessarily. Well, maybe they were...

Once:

At the Kiwanis welcome luncheon for new teachers, a burly horse rancher eyeballed me, taking notice of my Semitic features and long (long) black hair and said to me, "Schwartz, huh? That's yer name?" followed by: "'Bout time we have a Native American teachin' in our school." What? Huh? Never figured that one out, but it sure sounded like he meant well. Still does.

And then, a few months later, a student, Rory, upon seeing the Star of David hanging around my neck, exclaimed with great curiosity and unabashed enthusiasm: "Mr. Schwartz! I didn't know you're Jewish! Merry Christmas!"

Followed by his father, who, one day in spring, leaned on my classroom doorway cradling a bundle wrapped in bloody newspaper. "Here," he said, holding it out. "I'm obliged for teaching my boy to read." Turned out — after I had raced in terror to my principal with the bloody package — that it was venison. The boy's father had shot the animal for his family's food and wanted to share it with me. He had no money, but "venison was worth a whole lot more to him," my principal said.

Once:

There was Christopher, whose Mafia dad would come to teacher-parent conferences with two bodyguards and who hired a professional film crew to videotape commencement exercises and present a commemorative copy to every graduate.

And there was my teaching gig at an Orthodox yeshiva: One morning, several rabbis huddled in the corner of a hallway, presumably "davening." Not wanting to disturb their prayer, I walked quickly past them, but not so fast that I didn't hear them chuckling. Later, one of them confided that they were "debriefing" about the previous day's Howard Stern radio show.

Not long after that (having gone from Oregon to New York City licensed to teach CPR, as well as English), I asked my students to bring large dolls to class from their homes since I could not secure CPR dummies from the local Red Cross. Melissa raised her hand and, in a serious tone, informed that she no longer owned any dolls but that she would be happy to bring, on any day except Wednesday, her nanny.

About two years later, after I had moved on to another school, I received a phone call from Michael, who had been in Melissa's CPR class. Michael's father had recently had a heart attack at their dinner table. Michael wanted to tell me that he had applied CPR on his father and had resuscitated him just long enough to say, "I love you, Papa," before his father died.

And here, in Minneapolis, where I closed the book, there was Brad. Traditionally, we taught Chaucer's "The Canterbury Tales" at the end of each school year to our soon-to-be grads. Most got a kick out of reading the quite bawdy "The Miller's Tale." At one point in his tale, for reasons that you can investigate on your own, the miller explains that "Nicholas anon leet flie a fart." As we read this portion in proper Middle English (by the way, students can hardly believe the word "fart" existed in the 1300s), Brad let fly a tremendous (relevant) fart of his own, immediately eliciting a rousing standing ovation from his impressed and elated classmates.

And then, there was Cameron, my eighth-grader, who quite enthusiastically volunteered to read Shakespeare's sonnet 54 that offers the lovely sentiment, "O, how much more doth beauty beauteous seem." Cameron, quite unintentionally but with an emotional and sweet intonation, read, "Zero, how much more beauty beauteous seem." His classmates chose to ignore his snafu and not correct the sincere young man. Neither did I.

Or the students, bless their hearts, who chose to recite the "Tomorrow and tomorrow and tomorrow" soliloquy from "Macbeth" in Ukrainian, Chinese, French, Spanish, and Ewe. More beautiful, heartfelt renditions were never heard.

138

I hope we find more effective ways to keep wise, intelligent, good people teaching our kids.

Maybe we need to share more stories of the inevitable human and glorious moments.

Because it is a glorious profession.

On that Fateful November Day, Teacher Offered Lesson in Grace

Thanksgiving was approaching that November of 1963. During Beginning Spanish class, Senora De la Pena jubilantly orchestrates our usual repeat-after-me sentences, like: "Me llamoes." (My name is) First, we repeat in unison, sounding like an enthusiastic but way-off-key choir. Then Senora waltzes through the aisles and, with a graceful wave of her slender index finger, points at one of us to solo.

When it's my turn, I declare in a phony-sounding Spanish accent, "Me llamo es Ricardo," trying futilely to trill my r's. I love how Senora's voice and accompanying gestures urge us to recite so confidently and majestically as she sweeps her arms across her body and over and around her wavy black hair like she's conjuring our words to float magically back toward her. And her vibrant outfits! Amalgamations of indigos, magentas, royal blues, honeydews, and lemon yellows clash dramatically with her turquoise and silver jewelry and one of her many beautiful gossamer shawls. On this day, Senora wears the purple one.

In the spirit of Thanksgiving, our teacher also has us take turns

proclaiming: "Estoy agradecio por" ("I am thankful for"). If we don't know the Spanish word for what makes us grateful, she helps out. Most kids opt for the predictable mi perro, mi gato, mis amigos, mi familia. Heckie, the class wiseacre, says: "Estoy agradecio por Bonomo's Turkish Taffy."

Senora doesn't miss a beat. "Ah! Bonomo's Chicloso Turco, mi querido nino."

I want to offer a zany word, so she will smile and call me her dear boy, too.

But it doesn't happen.

That's because the intercom static that always precedes an announcement crackles to life. But instead of Principal Ellis, we hear the slightly quivering voice of a radio broadcaster. Even a 12-year-old can tell he's clinging to his composure as he describes Mrs. Kennedy grabbing the president and Catholic priests arriving at Parkland Hospital in Dallas. We wait anxiously for Senora to tell us what's happening. Instead, she walks into the hallway, then returns and collapses into her chair. Principal Ellis has switched off the broadcast, and he directs our teachers to "detain us" in our classrooms even after the dismissal bell. Staring at Senora, all we need is for her to reassure us this isn't really happening.

Instead, we watch her weep.

Senora rises unsteadily and summons us to stand and fold our hands like her. She recites what must have been a prayer in Spanish. Soon after, Principal Ellis instructs teachers to release all students to their next class.

You might remember that school was canceled across the nation the following Monday. I spent it worrying about the whys, what-ifs, and what-nows.

But upon our return to school after those grim days of mourning, something happened for which I have been forever thankful.

Senora greets each one of us at her classroom door with a hug. She's dressed in her usual blend of exotic colors. Today her gossamer shawl is white. She isn't her usual over-the-top exuberant self, but it's obvious she's determined to smile and encourage us to do the same.

We're heartened when she revives our individual "Estoy agradecio por…" proclamations, the ones that had been interrupted so cruelly a few days before. Even to her junior high horde of chronically confused pre-adolescents, Senora's message is clear: Despite unnerving and calamitous events that inevitably blindside our individual and collective lives, we will persevere, alone and together. Life goes on. The bloody package — that it was venison. The boy's father had shot the animal for his family's food and wanted to share it with me.

Ma'am was Tough — and I Should Have Thanked Her

Looking back, it seems all we did was study for Ma'am's tests, diagram her impossibly complex sentences and read, read, read. "She's a very good teacher, you know," my mother said.

"Why? Because she's so hard?"

"Partly. You should thank her."

"That'll be the day."

Friends and I obsessed over our teacher at sleepovers, on the school bus, at Plitman's Deli. Not because she was young, pretty, fun, and friendly. She wasn't.

In truth, she was curt and hardnosed and wore a perpetual frown, fuddy-duddy dresses, and those bleak black shoes that made a scary noise when she walked the aisles between our desks.

Mom's teacher-friend heard somewhere that Ma'am was married once, but something happened. I asked what and was told to mind my own business about such things.

Right. It triggered not-so-nice guesswork and gossip about her. We were eighth-graders, after all.

She demanded we address her as "Ma'am," not Miss or Mrs. so-and-so. So even beyond the classroom, she was "Ma'am" to us: "What'd you get on Ma'am's test?"

"Rose and her mom saw Ma'am riding a bike!"

"Ma'am recited all of 'Annabel Lee' without stopping. How does she do that?"

In fact, Ma'am could recite every poem she had us "dissect." When r-sounds appeared, she'd trill them theatrically — especially the alliterative ones. We'd roll our eyes and stifle our giggles. When she caught us in the act, she'd stop and stare with merciless tight lips for a 10 count at least. But her silent browbeatings were worth it. No one could trill their r's like Ma'am.

On the other hand, once she recited "To an Athlete Dying Young" in a way that brought at least one hotshot class jock near to tears. Another time Ma'am took us to the Guthrie Theater to see "The Glass Menagerie." She made a seating chart. I sat next to Martha, who cried during the last scene. Ma'am put her arm around Martha. I couldn't believe it.

We thought Ma'am was probably the planet's smartest person. It seemed she'd read every novel, poem, and play. Plus, she knew history, science, even math. She quoted from the Bible. She lectured without notes. She didn't hem and haw. She didn't make mistakes. Ma'am demanded succinctness. Once, trying to ingratiate myself to her, I said, "Boy, I studied really hard for this test, Ma'am." All that did was beget one of her no-nonsense mini-tutorials:

"Boy" is meaningless.

"Yes, Ma'am."

"'Really' is unnecessary to your point."

"Yes, Ma'am."

"Now, what did you do?"

"I studied hard for this test, Ma'am."

Ma'am was a notoriously hard grader. An A was a long shot. Legend had it a kid hyperventilated and wound up in the nurse's office after Ma'am gave him an "A+/Superior work."

Here's a sampling of grades Ma'am gave me on homework hoarded by my mother, stashed in a steamer trunk I inherited: "B/Do you intend to ever use their and there correctly?" (Know Your Homonyms worksheet); "C-/See me after class. Bring this with you."

("A Day in the Live [sic] of a [sic] Orangutane [sic]").

To say Ma'am was demanding understates it. On Recitation Friday, you'd better stand straight beside your desk, "hands out of your pockets," and recite your assigned poem mistake-free or "Do it again." Or again. (It took me several stabs at "Shall I compare thee to a summer's day?" to satisfy her.)

Was your homework sloppy, late, presumed lost, or, heaven help you, copied? Did you incorrectly diagram "Mary delivered the flower bouquet to her ailing grandmother on a rainy day"?

145

"Be here at 3:30. Make arrangements," she'd say.

One morning, Ma'am picked me to read aloud from Charles Dickens' "Great Expectations." Reading aloud at Ma'am's lectern was a huge deal to us, like she'd granted entrée into her sacrosanct space. Imagine an eighth-grade boy trying his damnedest to impress his teacher by mimicking the acerbic voice of Miss Havisham (remember her?), the novel's vengeful, jilted spinster:

"On this day of the year, long before you were born, this heap of decay... was brought here. It and I have worn away together. The mice have gnawed at it, and sharper teeth than teeth of mice have gnawed at me. When the ruin is complete... and when they lay me dead, in my bride's dress on the bride's table — which shall be done, and which will be the finished curse upon him — so much the better if it is done on this day!"

I must have nailed it. Otherwise, I never would have said, with such sophomoric chutzpah, "You remind me of Miss Havisham, Ma'am." While my classmates sat stone-cold silent, I remember trying to disguise my nasty slip-of-the-tongue with a fake guffaw. My plan was to apologize to Ma'am after class, accept a consequence (detention? some sort of reflective composition? our vice-principal's paddle?), and that would be that. It didn't turn out that way. My punishment was far worse. Ma'am took me into the dusty walk-in book room and said, "Your remark about me was

146

cruel. I thought you were a nice young man. But I was wrong." We still talk about Ma'am. Her r-trillings. Those shoes. How we feared her and revered her.

What a brilliant teacher she was.

But I never thanked her. Mom was right, I should have.

Keep It Interesting and Keep It Fun

You might have read that Tom Neiman, creator of the Southwest Minneapolis Community Education Program, is retiring.

Almost everyone calls him Neiman. He has outlasted six or eight (I've lost count) Minneapolis Public Schools superintendents and countless administrative types, none of who could match his staying and schmoozing power and uninterrupted success at enriching the minds and hearts of thousands of Twin City kids (and grownups) over four decades.

In a profession where the search for a better way is swayed by pendulum swings, spiffy acronyms, and the reinvention of the same ol' wheel, Neiman's approach to education has always been consistent and simple: Kids learn better when they play. Teachers teach better when they teach what they love. So keep it interesting, and keep it fun. Learning will follow.

On any summer day since 1983, you could walk into Southwest High School, where his Super Summer Program lives (for what seems like forever and will continue to) and become immersed in a world of happy campers, literally: kids learning woodworking, chess, and cooking, writing poetry, stumbling over their French, wrestling with math puzzles, rehearsing plays, playing Quidditch or hiking down the block to the lake to catch and toss back a sunfish or two.

And there in the middle of it all was Neiman, wearing some funny getup at the microphone and welcoming the kids (by name!) along with their astonished parents, who barely believed their children were getting this kind of bang for their buck for a whole day. A whole summer!

And what an eclectic array of classes!

How about Mock Trials: It's the law in the morning and Fishing – Minnows and Muskies in the afternoon? Or Dinosaurs: Dig Those Dinos after breakfast and How to be a Private Detective after lunch? And the next week? Try Room and Locker Décor and Harry Potter Adventures.

And all of this for how much? That's all? Are you kidding me? Not uncommon was it to hear a parent victoriously proclaiming to another that Neiman's Super Summer Camp was way more educational, inspiring and wondrous than the neighbor kid's daily two-hour bus schlep to and from Lake Whatever Day Camp. And for how much?

But that's not all. Neiman's Adult Community Education Program has been just as right brain/left brain-friendly for us oldsters.

Renowned since the '70s (that's right, the '70s) for its plethora of courses taught by professionals and laypeople like you and me, the evening classes, just like the kid versions, have always been predicated on Neiman's uncompromising premise: Keep it interesting and keep it fun.

So, to get to your classroom, you sometimes zigzagged through an onslaught of puppies and proud but sheepish owners in the main hallway during Puppy Training 1, or maybe you just wanted a cup of hot apple cider and a cookie on your way to Henna (Learn to mix, design, and apply henna), or for those so inclined, Chair Caning.

And always, there was Neiman, donned in his more business-like attire (apropos for the evening adult crowd) that never – ever – changed over the decades: a polyester, wide collar dress shirt and a mismatched '70s-era wide tie, not even close to reaching his belt buckle.

I'm pretty sure he was wearing the maroon paisley that one day in '74 when, as a fledging, newbie teacher, I asked him for a job in his program, and he gave me one, along with that ubiquitous cup of apple cider and prescription for success: "Make it interesting and make it fun."

That was 1974. It's 2016. Neiman has stood the test of time, circumvented the trendy demands for innovation and change (but not without a skirmish or two along the way), and held on tightly to his simple but not-so-easy-to-achieve expectation: There must be joy in learning.

No one knows this better than the thousands of kids who passed through his program and their parents who long ago were those kids — all of them, simply, Neiman's kids.

Spend time in any school, and you'll probably agree that change is inevitable and sometimes necessary, but here, in the world, according to Neiman, not trying to fix what never broke has made all the difference.

Well done, Neiman.

We Duck, Cover, Fear the Worst, but Life Goes On

Minneapolis students practiced a duck-and-cover drill in 1957, preparing for the possibility of a nuclear bomb attack.

Some of us remember those duck-and-cover drills in school: In anticipation of a nuclear bomb drop, kids in bygone days practiced diving underneath our desktops and covering our heads with our arms. We'd hide there ("No talking under there!") and wait for the "all clear" over the intercom.

I remember my overly large friend Hershey having a hard time with the duck-and-cover. He fretted over not having room enough to fit all of himself under his desk. Once, he was so afraid of exposing parts of his body, he burst into tears and cried, "Mrs. Feldman, I don't want to die."

Mrs. Feldman told him to hide the best he could. She and God would take care of him. I'm sure she was serious.

We were assured by a lot of grownups that the duck-and-cover would protect us from a nuclear bomb they seemed sure would come.

Most of us kids took this weekly rehearsal seriously. We'd been shown enough films and filmstrips of an exploding nuclear bomb and what it would do to us.

Even so, I remember how a few kids joked that a nuclear bomb explosion would make "monkey meat" out of us (whatever that meant). Thinking back, that was probably a façade for fears. And maybe not a bad way to cope.

Of course, the bombs didn't fall, and as time passed, we (mostly) came to believe the duck-and-cover had bordered on silliness.

Some of us even offered "monkey meat" jokes of our own and enjoyed making "ka-boom" sounds with our inflated cheeks — out of the teacher's earshot, of course.

Until that massive bullet that we dodged in 1962 when the very scary Russian Premier Nikita Khrushchev blinked first, dismantled his nuclear missile installations in Cuba, and our hero JFK sent him packing back to Russia. After that near-miss, even us kids understood how close we had come to disintegration. We knew then things would never be the same.

But life went on. Our parents seemed to know, to quote George Harrison, how to "cope with this heavy load," despite their apprehensions, as if they'd been there before. And they had: when a world war had deranged their daily lives and loved ones were lost. In the same way, we've tried to teach our own kids since the terrorist attacks of September 11, 2001.

And now, here we are again.

We have a pretty good idea of how to get through this pandemic. That we'll probably be living with it for a long time is sinking in. But if we play our cards right by thinking and behaving smartly, the time will come when we're up and running again — but not like before. Hopefully, when it's over, we'll reflect on our rational behavior (e.g., how we watched over our elderly neighbors and helped the helpless) and irrational behavior (e.g., how some hoarded toilet paper and bottled water as we allowed the collegians to spring-break on Florida beaches). And we'll prepare better for the next time.

Until then, I'm thinking longer and harder (for which I suddenly have plenty of time) about how every day for four years — every single day — my parents lived and breathed the fear of what might happen to them brought on by a world war.

I'm thinking about those weekly duck-and-cover drills and scared kids like my friend Hershey.

And I'll think more about our collective horrific witnessing of, and then courageous recovery from, 9/11 — and how after each crisis, life went on but was never the same.

Stewart Matches Randall-the-Enforcer's Gaze...

(A strange but sophisticated student I can't forget)

128,125. That's a pretty accurate estimate of the number of students I've taught over a bunch of decades. Around this time each autumn, at the beginning of a new school year, I think about some of them — Where are they? What are they doing? Did I serve them well as their teacher? — but there's one I think about most often. Stewart.

My hunch is every teacher has their "Stewart," just as all of us have a dominant memory of one teacher tucked away in our hearts and minds forever.

Stewart must be 30 by now. He was just 14 back then ...

He enters the classroom several minutes early as always — except for that one time. He stores his long, black umbrella underneath his front-row-center desk, unsnaps the metal clasps of his faux leather briefcase, and places a crisp, white legal pad and fountain pen in front of him. Soon, behind and next to him, other students take their seats, chattering away, ignoring Stewart's presence and precise preparations for the start of class. He seems light-years removed from them and oblivious to the friendly ruckus.

Only in a rare moment does Stewart chat with another classmate. He admits his disdain for the "riff-raff," as he once described them to me in confidence during one of our weekly lunches.

Yet, sometimes, for just a moment, Stewart's eyes hint that he might be another insecure, even lonesome 14-year-old when I catch him glancing at other students, then retreating into his notebook when he thinks they see him looking their way.

Stewart defines himself as an adult or, more precisely, a "scholar-entrepreneur." But the kids see him as strange, contrived, and oddly aloof. As one boy says, "He acts pretty dumb."

Stewart's persona is peculiar for sure, and I'm curious to know more about him. He eats alone in the cafeteria, and that's heart-wrenching to observe, so I invite him to join me for a weekly lunch in my office. His acceptance is formal but gracious, and I include the caveat that if he wants, we can discuss a shared reading that he might find intellectually stimulating. Stewart agrees.

I suggest John Steinbeck's "The Moon is Down" because of the story's reference to Socrates' "Apology," which I know he's reading on his own. I'm impressed that Stewart makes connections between the two works, particularly regarding the imminent executions of Socrates and Orden, the mayor of the Nazi-occupied town in the novella. Stewart seems moved by these characters' honor, courage, and devotion to their ideals and the acceptance of their imminent demise because of them.

Stewart reminds me that the novella's title comes from "Macbeth," which we are reading in class, when Banquo asks his doomed son, "How goes the night, boy?" and Fleance replies, "The moon is down. I have not heard the clock."

"I find that fascinating," Stewart says between sips of his Perrier. Stewart prepares for each lunch ritualistically, with the same precision he does for class: He always knocks lightly on my office door despite its being wide open. He selects the same chair at the round table and places his lunch box in front of him. He unfolds a crisp, clean white linen tablecloth, thoroughly flattening out any wrinkles. On it, he sets a small crystal-like glass, his mini-bottle of Perrier, and a small plate upon which he places his never-changing lunch: three isosceles-shaped white Cheddar cheese slices, a white-bread bologna sandwich, two slivers of green pepper, and a hermetically sealed cookie. Then, he fills his glass, raises it, and offers a toast to our "good health and fortune." I imagine the student hordes one floor below, gobbling their greasy pizza slices and leaving a trail of potato chip crumbs in the hallways. It's hard to imagine Stewart eating among them, although I wish he would.

***

157

A while back, I borrowed an idea from a colleague whereby any student tardy for the class is subjected to an innocuous punishment as determined by a democratically elected student, "Class Enforcer." Mildly embarrassing, silly sentences are decreed, just enough to create a deterrent for future tardies but always meant in the spirit of fun. One student was sentenced to act like a walrus and flap around the classroom. Another was sentenced to laugh hysterically at a pencil for 15 seconds, and so on.

The only time Stewart is tardy to class, I consider the possibility that I might need to intervene. Will the students demand that their Enforcer seize upon the chance to cross the line in this case? Stewart, after all, is easy pickings, and to some of his peers, he deserves a harsher sentence because of, well, who and what he is. And yet, if I did intervene, would that only widen the chasm between Stewart and his classmates?

"Sing a song," commands Randall-the-Enforcer.

Stewart matches Randall-the-Enforcer's gaze, ignoring the other students' nervous laughter. They, like me, are unsure how this drama will unfold. Stewart closes his briefcase nonchalantly, placing it and his ubiquitous umbrella under his desk. "What song would you like me to sing, Randall?" Stewart asks with calm resignation. I'm surprised and pleased that Stewart knows Randall's name. If there is a polar opposite of Stewart, it's this crude ruffian, Randall.

"Uh, what songs do you know?" Randall-the-Enforcer asks uneasily. Clearly, he hasn't anticipated Stewart's acquiescence and is caught off-guard.

"Randall, I know many songs."

Now, had Randall not been so flummoxed by Stewart's simple question, he might have recalled Stewart's reputation and snooty manner and commanded he sing something completely contrary to Stewart's lifestyle, as advised by two classmates: "Make 'im sing "Kiss Me Thru the Phone" advised Marshall. "No way," argues Rebel. (Honestly, his name was "Rebel".) "He should sing "Let's All Sing Like the Birdies Sing!" Instead, Randall-the-Enforcer condemns Stewart to sing "The Star-Spangled Banner." The class groans in opposition to such an uninspired, banal choice.

Whereupon Stewart rises, faces the class, waits for silence, and executes his punishment for tardiness by singing the entire national anthem with operatic bravado and patriotic zeal:

Oh, say can you see by the dawn's early light

What so proudly we hailed at the twilight's last gleaming...

The class responds with an odd mixture of eye-rolling, guffaws, and confused delight. But Stewart silences them with a slightly raised arm, which they quickly obey, including Randall, and he proceeds thusly in an unwavering, forceful, and melodic voice, singing the next four stanzas in their entirety and by heart:

...On the shore, dimly seen through the mists of the deep, Where the foe's haughty host in dread silence reposes, What is that which the breeze, o'er the towering steep,

As it fitfully blows, half conceals, half discloses...

...Their blood has washed out their foul footsteps' pollution. No refuge could save the hireling and slave

From the terror of flight, or the gloom of the grave: And the star-spangled banner in triumph doth wave O'er the land of the free and the home of the brave! Oh! Thus be it ever, when freemen shall stand Between their loved home and the war's desolation... And the star-spangled banner in triumph shall wave O'er the land of the free and the home of the brave!

***

Later that spring, Stewart informs me at lunch of his plan to attend a renowned East Coast prep school the next fall, where, he says, "I won't have to contend with the riff-raff because there isn't any." However, later I learned via the faculty grapevine that he had been rejected. Instead, he has enrolled at another school near us.

160

When learning that Stewart has transferred, some students are surprised. A few seem amused. Others are confused and even insulted. But many are disappointed. Erin laments, "He was strange, but he was really smart and kind of cool. How come he left? Didn't he like us?"

I never heard about Stewart after that, except recently when one of his classmates told me she thought she heard he had started a homemade cookie franchise out East. I just don't know.

But I think of him often, as you can see, and mostly now at each beginning of a school year.

On Banning Books

A Florida parent wants his child's school to remove a memoir written for young adult readers that includes the word "penis." Another wants Ray Bradbury's "Fahrenheit 451," his dystopian novel about book banning, banned. Another wants "opposing perspectives" to evolution, and global warming required teaching in science classes.

No kids of your own? That's OK. Their state legislature passed a bill this year allowing residents in any school district, "regardless of whether she or she has a child in school", a hearing before an "outside mediator" if they disapprove of what is or isn't being taught.

This revitalized book banning talk reminds me of these incidents during my teaching career…

Against the advice of a more experienced colleague, I choose Dalton Trumbo's gut-wrenching anti-war novel, "Johnny Got His Gun," to read with my students.

We begin with my reading to them: "Book 1: The Dead."

Me: "…It sounded like it was ringing in a room about a million miles wide. His head was a million miles wide too. To hell with the telephone. That damn bell must be at the other side of the world…"

I stumble through these two sentences because some words have been blacked out with a permanent marker. Guess which ones.

Student: "My book is all marked up." Another student: "Mine, too."

Me: "Raise your hand if your book has words blacked out." Everyone raises a hand. I flip deeper into my book. More words are blacked out. Then I get to what should have been Chapter XIV. It's not there.

After school, I searched the school library for a clean copy, but the librarian says she removed it from the shelf. That night I bought one at the bookstore. I read the targeted words: damn, hell, goddamn, sons-of-bitches, dirty bastards, for Christ's sake – just in Chapter I. As for Chapter XIV, to summarize: A young American soldier, Joe Bonham, horribly maimed and disfigured in battle during World War I, is lying in a hospital bed, his arms and legs amputated,

his face blown apart. He has no means to communicate with his caregivers. Then, about midway in the chapter, the narrator implies that Bonham's compassionate nurse masturbates him: ("Her hands sought out the far parts of his body. They inflamed his nerves with a kind of false passion that fled in little tremors along the surface of his skin.")

The next morning I seek out Miss Willow, our department chair and matriarch of the English Department, and ask about the censored pages. She has no concern, explaining that "our parents" don't want their children exposed to inappropriate words and descriptions "of things that might give them ideas." Besides, she adds, those words and discarded pages "don't add much to the story." I argue that the school wilted under parent pressure. Miss Willow counters it isn't censoring, "... since students are allowed to read the novel, aren't they?"

The next day I explain to my students that I'll be reading the "missing parts" to them; however, if anyone feels uncomfortable, they may leave the classroom. No one leaves.

The next day the books are confiscated, and I receive a letter of reprimand from the principal.

The Tale of How I Stopped Switching Majors

"You know, the smallest thing can change a life. In the blink of an eye, something happens by chance — and when you least expect it... into a future you never imagined."

Nicholas Sparks

In college, I switched majors umpteen times. Mostly on a whim. Many of my friends somehow knew their destiny from the get-go: business, law, advertising, journalism, dentistry...

I didn't. I was well-intentioned, but in the way, some flaky first-years and sophomores are (hence the term of Greek origin: sophos (wise), and mōros (foolish, dull, i.e., moron).

I tried animal husbandry, right after I'd decorated State Fair horse stalls and pig pens with crepe paper and bunting; political science, because our professor inserted Bob Dylan, Joan Baez, and Woody Guthrie lyrics into her lectures; psychology, because I'd trained Stanley, my Psych 103 lab rat, to deposit marbles in a tin can.

This went on for nearly two years. To Dad, I was frittering away my future and the "outrageous" $150 per quarter tuition. My excitement about operant conditioning (I think it was) and my and Stanley's successful feat was the last straw. Dad had had it and suggested that "maybe college isn't the right place for you right now."

That's when I proclaimed my intention to "go premed." "Mazel tov! Now you're making sense," Dad replied.

Of course, I wasn't making sense. I'd barely passed 10th-grade biology. Both of us neglected to consider that.

ADVERTISEMENT.

About the same time, I'd landed an on-campus job with the University of Minnesota vending services. Before sunrise, I'd load a van with candy, chips, soft drinks, pastries, plastic-wrapped white bread sandwiches, and cigarettes. I'd drive around campus all day and restock vending machines.

You couldn't beat the perks: driving the van to my classes, parking it in convenient "official vehicle only" spots; supplying grateful housemates with "leftovers"; and my favorite, offering pretty classmates door-to-door service to their next classes.

One morning at the beginning of winter term, a girl (Jodi)waited while I restocked pastries at Wilson Library. I gifted her a cherry Danish and offered her a ride to her class.

On the drive across the Washington Avenue bridge to the East Bank, we small-talked:

"What class?"

"I've got Chaucer now."

166

"Come again?"

"Chaucer. You know. The poet."

I pretended to know all about Chaucer. I remember vividly how bogus it sounded, especially when I casually mentioned that Chaucer was "far-out."

"But I'm premed," I added.

"You should take it anyway. We could study together." That's when I enrolled in Chaucer.

To pass the class, you had to memorize and recite, to Professor Kendahl's satisfaction, the first 34 lines of "The Canterbury Tales" in its original Middle English.

You know, it begins this way:

Whan that Aprille with his shoures soote,

The droghte of March hath perced to the roote, And bathed every veyne in swich licóur

Of which vertú engendred is the flour

It seemed impossible. But Jodi was smart, and she helped me. After acing her recitation, she briefed me: "Kendahl seats you in his armchair. If he offers you water, take it. When he says, 'Begin,' speak up. When you're done, he'll tell you your grade. Don't argue. And heads up. Hardly anyone gets an A."

My appointment to recite was on a snowy, late Friday afternoon. "Water?" (Thank you.)

"Begin."

167

"Whan that Aprille with his shoures soote,

The droghte of March hath perced to the roote... I stumbled from beginning to end."

"You can do better," said the professor. "Try again."

"Whan that Aprille..."

"Better. C-minus."

I felt the fool and was about to make a quick, woebegone exit when Professor Kendahl said, "You know, Mr. Schwartz, line nine is one of the most lyrical in English literature. What's your opinion?"

Then he chanted, "And smale foweles maken melodye," several times, waving his pipe like a conductor's baton and encouraging me to join in. I did. It was a charming, kooky, hypnotic moment — and best of all, unexpected.

So was his goodbye. Despite my clumsy, monotonic C-minus, Professor Kendahl shook my hand.

He shook my hand.

By then, Northrop Mall was winter-quiet and beautiful. Lamps lit the walkways like night lights.

" ...In the blink of an eye and when you least expect it into a future you never imagined..."

The following Monday, for the last time, I switched my major. "English?" said Dad with a flummoxed expression. "For crying out loud, son. Where will that get you?"

"I'll be a teacher."

It worked out pretty well.

Speaking of "bawdy…"

When I begin reciting the Prologue to Geoffrey Chaucer's "The Canterbury Tales" in Middle English ("Here bygynneth the Book of the Tales of Canterbury: Whan in April with his shoures soote…") so also begins my students' bellyaching about why they "hafta read this."

Despite their grousing, we dived (or belly-flopped) into our abridged study of Chaucer, starting with a mini-lesson on Middle English pronunciation and followed by the reading of just two of the many tales, told by Chaucer's patchwork of characters making their 14th-century pilgrimage to the shrine of St. Thomas Becket, who regale each other in a contest of storytelling to pass the time.

First, "The Wife of Bath's Tale": Chaucer describes her as "gap-toothed," which for some reason back then suggested a woman's sensuality and insatiable lust. My students like this, as demonstrated by their earnest examination of one another's teeth alignments. Next, the headliner, "The Miller's Tale," whose story, Chaucer warns the reader, might seem to some a bit raunchy. Hearing that, even my back-row dozers perk up.

What follows below brought not an ounce of concern from parents. So why do I include it in this discussion? Because in Florida, it now seems reasonable to think these two words could generate a hearing "before an outside mediator." Could it happen here in Minnesota, too?

Sex and flatulence.

There is increasing buy-in as my students read deeper into the Miller's tale of sex, trickery, more sex, a prank gone wrong (or right, depending upon your point of view), and more sex. But the deal is sealed for all when for reasons you can investigate on your own, the Miller tells his fellow pilgrims:

…This Nicholas anon leet flie a fart

As greet as it had been a thonder-dent …

Just when Cassie B. reads these lines in proper-sounding Middle English (By the way, the students can hardly believe the word fart existed in the 1300s), Charley, maybe in cahoots with Cassie, let's fly his own perfectly synchronized blast of flatulence. His impressed and elated classmates reward Charley with a rousing standing ovation.

Clearly, they understand Middle English.

But I think we have to do more than just hope that a parent or resident doesn't get wind of "The Miller's Tale" and attempt to ban students from this work's joy and wisdom. I believe now more than before that it could more easily happen, along with the works of, say, Toni Morrison, Charles Darwin, Harper Lee, Dalton Trumbo,

J.K. Rowling, Ray Bradbury, and of course, Mark Twain, whose classic "Huck Finn" was, not many years ago, banned from a school in Virginia – Mark Twain Intermediate School.

How Do You Spell 'Gratitude'?

"Good teachers will find a way to ... make things more interesting for their students. It requires a little more work, a little more imagination, and maybe even a little acting ability. The best teachers make learning interesting, exciting and important. The teachers who do that well deserve our support and most of all our gratitude."

Alfred Thompson, educator

Mr. West's determination to make good spellers out of us was legendary. He'd tell us: "Good and poor spelling sends a message."

What such messages were was fuzzy to us back then. We were 12. But a "spelling" grade on our report cards was a clear reality. And even as 12-year-olds, we could recognize and admire, and would work our tails off for, any teacher who had an authentic passion for a subject.

So spelling became a mighty big deal to us.

Twenty-four words each week, one practice test and one "for all the marbles," Mr. West would warn us. Pens, not pencils, were mandatory, and no cross-outs were allowed on the all-the-marbles test.

I'm looking at some of my test papers now (my mother saved everything). On one, my score and grade were indicated as: "21/24/C." I'd missed "innocent," "majority" and "historical" — the latter because I didn't dot one of the i's.

Mr. West didn't teach spelling rules. "Memorize and use the words on the list like you own them," he'd tell us. We earned an extra point for underlining any of that week's words that we fanatically searched for in the newspaper. If you delivered a restaurant menu to him with a misspelled word, you were hailed a hero, with Mr. West leading the cheers. (Intentional misspellings like "x-tra" irked him the most.)

Above all, each word we incorporated into our assignments earned us more points. But there were risks. I have an English assignment in which we were asked to describe our parents. I used a word from that week's list — "intimate" (which might have made Mr.

West chuckle) — but spelled it "intimat." He deducted a point from the following week's test.

Lesson learned.

Years later, I somehow fell two credits short of graduating on time from the University of Minnesota. To help me out, one of my English professors, Martin Steinmann, agreed to an independent study. All I had to do was turn in a paper on a topic of my choosing. Naturally, I chose Shakespeare to impress him.

I barely recall writing it but remember thinking it turned out swell. I'd never know how swell, though, because I'd spelled Shakespeare — "Shakespear" — 36 times. I know this number because Steinmann returned the paper to me with an angry-looking red "FAIL" written underneath this: "You misspelled Shakespeare 36 times. You might ask yourself why." He had circled each of my offenses.

Lesson learned.

In graduate school, Richard Welton, professor of anatomy and physiology, was just as demanding about correct spelling as Mr. West and Prof. Steinmann had been. On exams, he deducted half a point for each misspelled term. To Prof. Welton, it wasn't enough to know the whereabouts and functions of the brachiocephalic vein, cerebellum, and arachnoid villi (all of which I misspelled). This drove many students batty. Once, he told my study partner, a whining phlebotomist wannabe, that he wouldn't trust anyone with his own blood if he knew that person was a careless speller.

Prof. Welton's merciless reputation for demanding correct spelling of his students — and himself — was well-deserved. One day he delayed his lecture to apologize after a student pointed out in the written instructions for that week's lab — "Graded synaptic resistance, irradiation of reflexes, synaptic fatigue, forms of nerve stimuli" — the only spelling gaffe (legend has it) that Prof. Welton ever made:

"Decapatate a frog as directed by your instructor."

Along with the apology, he awarded every student a bonus half-point on the next exam. This "touché" elicited a lovely, good-natured cheer. He awarded the student who detected the misspelling a full extra point, which compensated neatly for his misspelled (but correct) answers to numbers 5: "tribeculaer [sic] carnae" and 34: "visceral efferant [sic] nerves." That student was my study partner. Toward the end of the term, Prof. Welton offered us the opportunity to "buy back" points we'd lost for the misspellings if we donated a pint of blood at the local blood drive. Many years after he'd retired from 35 years of teaching anatomy and physiology, I learned that he himself had donated blood 230 times in his lifetime. And that's how I was taught to be a good speller.

Made in the USA
Monee, IL
11 May 2022

96255898R00105